WELLINGTON'S SCAPEGOAT

by the same author

*Kitchener's Sword-Arm: The Life and Campaigns of
General Sir Archibald Hunter*

*A Life of Sir John Eldon Gorst:
Disraeli's Awkward Disciple*

WELLINGTON'S SCAPEGOAT

THE TRAGEDY OF LIEUTENANT-COLONEL CHARLES BEVAN

by

ARCHIE HUNTER

With a foreword by

GENERAL SIR MICHAEL ROSE

LEO COOPER

Dedicated to the descendants of Charles and Mary
Bevan and especially to the memory of Major James
Bevan and Anne Colfer

First published in Great Britain in 2003 by
LEO COOPER
an imprint of Pen & Sword Books
47 Church Street, Barnsley, South Yorkshire, S70 2AS

ISBN 1 84415 029 1

Typeset in 13/14.75pt Garamond by
Phoenix Typesetting, Auldgirth, Dumfriesshire

Printed in England by
CPI UK

Contents

Maps

Introduction and Acknowledgements

The dramatic escape in May 1811 during the Peninsular War of 1,000 Frenchmen from the encircled garrison of Almeida in Portugal is well known to historians and to students of the war. It is also known that Wellington blamed, for what he perceived to be a major disaster, the young commanding officer of the 4th Foot (The King's Own Royal Regiment), Lieutenant-Colonel Charles Bevan. To Wellington's fury Bevan and his men were not present, as ordered, to defend the important bridge at Barba del Puerco over which the garrison made its escape. Bevan, believing himself and his regiment to have been unjustly blamed by Wellington for the escape, requested an inquiry, a request which Wellington refused.

The untimely death of Bevan in the Portuguese town of Portalegre two months after the episode described has also been alluded to by historians but until recently virtually nothing has been known about Bevan and his life. This has changed with the discovery among the Bevan family papers of some eighty letters which Bevan wrote to his wife in 1804/1811 while abroad or on campaign in the French revolutionary wars.

This book aims to break new ground by

- telling the story of Bevan's life and examining his character and military capabilities;
- analysing the circumstances of the escape of the French garrison and of the part played by the 4th Foot, in the light of the orders issued by Wellington, in trying to prevent it.

I am grateful for the permission I have received to use and quote from unpublished copyright and other material in the care of the Museum of the King's Own Royal Regiment at Lancaster; the Museum of the 15th/19th The King's Royal Hussars at Newcastle-upon-Tyne; the National Library of Scotland; the Public Record Office at Kew; Soldiers of Gloucestershire Museum at Gloucester, and the owners of both the Bevan papers and the manuscript of Georgina Bevan's unpublished novel about the life of Charles Bevan.

This book would not have been written but for the inspiration of William Colfer whose late wife Anne was a direct descendant of Charles Bevan. It was he who collected together and then transcribed the Bevan letters. For the enthusiastic help he has given me in many different ways, including research, I am most grateful. He also read and commented on my manuscript as have both my brother David Hunter and Colonel Gerald Napier. Their trouble and valuable advice has been greatly appreciated. I am also indebted to Rear-Admiral Tom Bradley and Captain Guy Crowden for their guidance on certain naval matters, to Iain Fletcher for alerting me to the article written many years ago by the historian S.G.P. Ward on the escape of the garrison from Almeida, to Michael Ponting for his expert contribution with regard to the production of some of the illustrations and to both Wendela Schurmann and Paddy McCrimmon for the work they did on some of the French aspects of my book.

Other very useful help and advice was kindly given by Sigrún Appleby, Dr Iain Brown, Principal Curator, Department of Manuscripts, National Library of Scotland; the staff of Crewkerne Library; Emily Davis of the National Army Museum; Peter Donnelly, Curator, King's Own Royal Regiment Museum; Sir John Gorst; Elyn W. Hughes; my son Archie Hunter and his son Archie; Henry Keown-Boyd; my granddaughter Georgia Mann; Gwen McClay; Oriel Art; Dr Paulo Lowndes Marques; Claud Rebbeck; George Streatfeild; Ralph Thompson; Allison Wareham and Dr C.M. Woolgar, Head of Special Collections at the Hartley

Library, University of Southampton. I am also grateful to Tom Hartman for his invaluable guidance as editor.

There cannot be too many authors these days who laboriously write out their texts in longhand, but I am one of them. This strange habit did not deter our old friend Lorna Kingdon from producing a beautiful typescript of my work. My profound thanks go to her. As always my final word is for my wife Mirabel. She has once again valiantly accepted the role of author's factotum. I cannot thank her enough for her enduring patience and sound advice.

Archie Hunter
Church House, Winsham

February, 2003

Foreword

by

General Sir Michael Rose

The tragic story of Charles Bevan is not well known and its telling reminds us that, in the confused circumstances of war, it is indeed a thin line that separates a hero from someone who will forever be condemned by history as a failure. Following the bloody defeat of the French under Marshal Masséna at Fuentes de Oñoro, a battle that took place on 3–5 May 1811 and one that was deemed by the Iron Duke to be one of the most difficult battles of the entire Peninsula Campaign, Wellington attempted to prevent the subsequent evacuation of the nearby town of Almeida by the French. His specific orders were that the bridge over the River Agueda at Barba del Puerco should be seized in order to block the escape route of the French. These orders were despatched to Major-General Sir William Erskine who was dining at the time he received them but who failed to pass them on immediately. Much later that night General Erskine finally did give the necessary orders to Lt Col Charles Bevan commanding the 4th Regiment to march on the bridge. However, Charles Bevan and his Regiment arrived in situ too late and, as a result of this unfortunate and entirely unneccessary delay, most of the French garrison of Almeida were able to cross the undefended bridge at Barba del Puerco and so rejoin the main French army.

The Duke of Wellington was of course exceedingly irritated by this gross disregard of his orders and the subsequent escape of the French, and wrote: 'The business would have been different if we had caught the garrison of Almeida'. He was also deeply frustrated by the overall quality of his British generals in relation to those of the French and a scapegoat was needed. However, Sir William Erskine made quite sure that the blame did not fall on himself, but on the unfortunate Charles Bevan. This notwithstanding the fact that Wellington had no time for Erskine who had already been sacked once and who many of his contemporaries considered to be not only mad but also 'blind as a beetle'.

Much of the evidence that has been gathered for this book is from contemporary eyewitness accounts written during the Peninsular War. They give a fresh insight into the hardships and difficulties endured by all those serving in Wellington's Army at that time. Nevertheless his soldiers, including Charles Bevan, greatly admired Wellington and forgave him his mistakes, even though they often cost lives.

The demands of war and the qualities required by commanders and soldiers on the 21st century battlefield remain much the same as they were two hundred years ago. Sadly, today there is more of a blame culture in our nation. This tends to undermine the essential qualities of mental toughness and sense of service and duty among our citizens, qualities that will surely be needed if in the future we are to win wars as Wellington was able to do. This book offers us a useful and timely glimpse of another, more honourable, era that modern soldiers might do well to imitate.

Michael Rose

Prologue

A temporary halt in a miserable village called Nave de Aver gives me time to inform my dearest Mary that Ld Wellington's Army continues still in close pursuit of the French who are now almost out of Portugal. Two hours march carried us into Spain; we are but 4 Leagues from Ciudad Rodrigo (about 12 English miles). It is reported that they have thirty thousand men on the banks of the Agueda a river that divides these two countries. Or nearly so – just to the north. They disputed the passage of the [River] Coa and we had some loss. Theirs, however, was much more severe. The 5th Division were ordered to drive a [French] Corps from their position. But that Corps moved off as we advanced upon them. The 4th Regt. have not yet fired a shot! I indeed thought that on that day we should have come in for our share of laurel; but the enemy would not give us the opportunity although they waited till we were within a few hundred paces of them.[1]*

Thus wrote, in early April 1811, Charles Bevan, commanding officer of the first battalion of the 4th Regiment of Foot, to his wife Mary. He was on campaign in Portugal and had been away from home for 15 months. Mary Bevan and her four small children were

* See Notes on p 189

1

living at Money Hill, the house of her mother in the then rural backwater of Rickmansworth in Hertfordshire. Charles, a dutiful husband, wrote regularly to Mary, who was now following avidly the progress of Lord Wellington's army as it vigorously chased Marshal Masséna's troops through central Portugal towards Spain. Proud of her soldier husband, Mary awaited Charles' letters with an eagerness which was only matched by his impatience for news of home and family.

While the 4th Regiment, part of the 5th Division, was as anxious as any other regiment in the army to hammer the enemy, to Bevan's dismay his men had not yet seen any action. Then in May Mary had a letter from Charles after the battle of Fuentes de Oñoro up on the Spanish frontier. He wrote:

> We have, my dearest Mary, now been seven days perched upon these hills opposite the French Army under Massena hourly expecting to engage; on the 5th there took place a very [illegible] affair on the right. The Enemy was repulsed in his attempt to turn our right flank with considerable loss, that on our side was also severe, but I do not know really what: report says from 12 to 1300 killed & wounded. The attack on the part of the Enemy was chiefly made by Cavalry, all beastly drunk. Our Division is on the left where they only skirmished & wounded about 35 or 40 men. The Light Companies only were engaged, that of the 4th fortunately did not lose a man. We are just now quite at a loss to guess what the Enemy are about, it was yesterday reported that they were on the retreat, but whether to make their attack on another part of the line or to fall back has not yet been properly ascertained. However do what they can, they must be beaten. The Army is in high Spirits & confident of success.[2]

A few days later, on 15 May, Charles told his wife that, after much marching and counter-marching, they had had a skirmish with the French garrison of the fortress of Almeida on their retreat. But he said they were 'unfortunately a little too late to do more than what you will see in the Papers took place – their escape is a matter of great annoyance to us all'. This 'escape' was to become a matter of major importance in Bevan's story, as we shall see.

The next month found Bevan and his regiment, still with the 5th Division, hastening to the south to join Wellington who was by then besieging Badajoz. Charles kept Mary posted of their progress on the march, and on 10 June he wrote from Sabugal saying they would before long be crossing the Tagus and

> proceed to the neighbourhood of Badajoz where it appears the enemy will collect a large force – there are a thousand rumours in consequence of this, some saying that they [the French] are going to evacuate Spain, others that they are going to fight a great fight . . . I hope we shall at last come in for our share of what is going on.[3]

Nine days later at Castelo Branco they were expecting

> an order to join the main body of the army. We hear many and varied reports, however it is certainly believed that [Marshal] Soult is advancing in force, what is to be the consequence of this it is not easy to judge. I am very tired of this marching backwards and forwards – our men get badly off for shoes and it occupies all our time to try and provide new articles of equipment. I say try because I can not always succeed.[4]

At last, towards the end of June, the 5th Division reached its destination in the south and early the next month Bevan's regiment fell back on the pleasant town of Portalegre. Here he wrote a letter dated 4 July complaining how uncomfortably hot it was and how his men were feeling the effect of the heat. He went on to tell Mary that he had been hoping to see Major Charles Paterson, his brother-in-law, serving not far away with the 28th Regiment (Charles was married to Mary's sister Eleanor) but he had been frustrated in his plans after receiving an order to march. In any case his only horse had a sore back. He ended by saying that he had nothing to tell her except he was 'very much fatigued'[5]. There was a brief postscript to say that he would write to Caroline [his sister] in a day or two.

This was the last letter Mary was ever to receive from Charles. Four days after writing it he was dead.

News of her husband's death must have come as a terrible shock to Mary. There had been, it was well known, a lull in the fighting, and Charles' health had been good. Eventually she was told the following: on the evening of 5 July Charles had been seized with a 'violent fever'. He had apparently become delirious, a condition lasting with some intermission for two days. At first the doctors were not unduly alarmed but then pronounced him to be suffering from a disorder 'of the bile producing an inflammation of the stomache'. When the delirium subsided he was 'too insensible to speak to anyone' but at the same time did not seem to be in pain, only being in a 'kind of stupor'.[6] On the morning of 8 July he died.

Mary had been given details of her husband's sudden death by Major John Piper, the second in command of the 4th Regiment and by Charles Paterson. Colonel Henry Torrens, Military Secretary at the Horse Guards in London, had also been in touch with the family. Then, some months later, Captain James Dacres of the Royal Navy, Mary's brother, (he had been serving in the West Indies that July) told his sister that Paterson had been trying to learn the name of the surgeon who had treated Charles during his illness. He was doing this evidently at Mary's request, but, so Dacres said, there were difficulties.[7] No wonder, for Mary had been deceived by the account of the circumstances of Charles' death. They were, in fact, a total fabrication.

CHAPTER ONE

The Mediterranean

Charles Bevan was born on 4 October 1778, the eldest of four children, whose parents were Thomas and Ann. The family lived in comfortable circumstances in Ashtead in Surrey. Thomas Bevan, whose family had originally come from Carmarthen in West Wales, was a businessman. He had prospered in his career and, besides the house in Surrey, he owned another one in Harley Street in central London. He had been sufficiently confident in his status to take out, in middle age, a grant of arms. Of Ann's forbears we know nothing except that her mother was often referred to as 'old Mrs Walton'. When Thomas died he left his wife modestly well off. As a widow she lived in nearby Beddington with her two unmarried daughters, Caroline and Juliana, known as Julia. Her sons had left home at an early age to pursue their careers: Charles as a soldier and Edward in the East India company.

It was decided when he was a boy that Charles should go into the army, though whether this was through his own choice or was at his father's wish we can only speculate. Accordingly in April 1795, when he was just 16½ years old, Charles became, by purchase, an ensign in the 37th Regiment of Foot, the forerunner of the North Hampshire regiment. In many ways Charles had got off to a flying start in life. He had received a good education and came from the kind of thriving middle-class background which bred confidence and a sense of initiative An ensign, earning 4s 8d per day, stood at the bottom rung of the ladder of commissioned officers. Promotion to Lieutenant would depend normally on a vacancy occurring and on money to purchase that vacancy. At about this time some two-thirds of commissions in the army were held by purchase.[1] As we shall see, Charles was never without funds to buy his promotion. To climb the ladder of advancement it was also of course invaluable for the young officer to come from the right background, preferably aristocratic or landed gentry, and to know the right people. Charles did not have these benefits and had therefore to rely on his own initiative and force of character. Certainly he did not lack intelligence, ambition or push. These traits were to serve him well, and he would go for opportunities whenever he saw them. The first came soon enough, and within less than six months of joining the 37th he was appointed lieutenant. He was at once posted to serve with his regiment in Gibraltar where he remained for nearly three years. Gibraltar, although regarded as an unhealthy station, maintained a considerable garrison of British troops. Indeed in peacetime in the eighteenth century there was often as many regiments of foot there as there would be in England.[2] This is not so surprising considering the strategic importance of Gibraltar since its capture by Admiral Rooke in 1704.

It is worth observing that even at this early stage, Charles had some characteristics that were not necessarily associated with the young fighting soldier. For instance, with something of the intellectual in his make-up, he was serious-minded, even bookish, and somewhat introverted. Nor was he, though personable, at heart a sociable man, even if he went through the motions adequately enough when required to. Nevertheless he pursued with some dedication a career which demanded courage and powers of endurance, qualities he did not lack.

For adventurous young Englishmen – and Bevan was one – the army at the end of the eighteenth century offered exciting opportunities after Europe had been plunged into a state of turmoil by the French Revolution. The one European power remaining steadfastly opposed to the military aggression of France was Britain, sometimes on her own but more often in coalition with other countries. Britain, with her growing Empire, relied on the power of the Royal Navy to defend her shores and far-flung trading posts and possessions. Nevertheless, her army, to meet the French threat, was being expanded. Thus in 1793 its strength was just under 43,000. Eight years later the figure was 160,000.[3] During the long years of Bonaparte's dominance in Europe the British army became involved, often outside Europe, in numerous expeditions against the French. Some of them were ill-considered and many were unsuccessful or at best of limited strategic value, until Wellington was firmly established in the Iberian peninsula in 1809.

By the end of 1795 France had overcome Holland and had annexed Belgium and all Germany up to the Rhine, besides regaining those parts of the country temporarily lost due to the intervention of powers hostile to the revolution. Turning to the young Corsican general of artillery who had saved the government on the streets of Paris in 1796, the ruling French Directory appointed Napoleon that year as commander of its revolutionary army in Italy. At once displaying his military genius, Napoleon proceeded to rout the forces of the Kingdom of Sardinia in Piedmont and then to defeat the Austrians the following year. The Directory, now anxious to keep Napoleon away from Paris after his exploits in Italy, invited the young general to invade England. He considered this possibility, but, prudently enough, rejected it. Instead he turned his eyes to the eastern end of the Mediterranean and beyond. Accordingly in 1798 he set sail for Egypt with the intention of undermining British influence there and, with his wide-ranging ambitions, of proceeding on to India, where, he considered, he might find the Mahrattas as sympathetic allies against the British presence. He captured Malta, arrived at Alexandria, defeated the Mameluke rulers of Egypt and entered Cairo in triumph. But he had forgotten Nelson, and his further plans in the region were frustrated when the French fleet was destroyed at the Battle of the Nile in August 1798. The French army, however, remained in Egypt, though Napoleon himself returned to France.

With the keen interest in current affairs he always displayed, Bevan had been contemplating events in Egypt from the other end of the Mediterranean, even though news of them travelled slowly. He had by now found himself a vacancy in the 28th Regiment of Foot (later the North Gloucestershire Regiment) and was able to purchase his promotion to captain in March 1800. The 28th was a famous regiment, whose origins went back to Gibson's Regiment of Foot raised in Portsmouth in 1694 and which became the 28th in 1751 after a 23-year span of duty in Ireland. Some years later, sword in hand, General James Wolfe, at the head of the 28th, found immortality one September day when scaling the Heights of Abraham, an assault which led to the capture of Quebec. In 1778 the Regiment played an active part in seizing St Lucia – the French were still the enemy – in what the regimental history describes as a brilliant episode. At one moment a heroic British force of 1,300 men, including the 28th, defeated 12,000 French.[4]

Bevan was now about to embark on a period of more active soldiering in this famous regiment. Probably his duties in Gibraltar, essentially garrison ones, did not give him, with his somewhat impatient temperament, enough to do. He had, however, managed during his time in Gibraltar to serve six months on the staff of General William Grinfield as his ADC. At first sight this might appear to be the kind of appointment unsuitable for someone like Bevan who lacked commitment to the social life. On the other hand Bevan had charm and was efficient. In any case he always liked being at the centre of events, even if those involving a young ADC in the garrison at Gibaltar were not likely to offer much drama. Nevertheless this experience as an ADC would serve him in good stead.

The Commanding Officer of his new regiment was 24-year-old Lieutenant-Colonel the Hon. Edward Paget, the fourth son of Lord Uxbridge. Paget is generally acknowledged to have been an outstanding soldier and leader of men. Already a veteran of several campaigns, he was to continue to have a dramatic career as a soldier, serving in Egypt, Sicily, Portugal and Spain. In 1809 he had the misfortune to lose an arm during the capture of Oporto and then in 1812, soon after being appointed as Wellington's second in command, to be taken prisoner while on a reconnaissance. At the end of his career his name was suggested as a possible Commander-in-Chief. Bevan came to know Paget well, and to look upon him as his mentor. For his part Paget almost certainly helped Bevan obtain promotion once, if not twice.

During the summer of 1800 Bevan spent some time with his regiment in Minorca. The capital, Port Mahon, was, with its harbour, of importance to the navy in its task of controlling the western Mediterranean and watching the French fleet at Toulon. It was also a valuable base for British troops. The island, originally Spanish, had had a checkered history during the eighteenth century changing hands between the French and British several times. The unfortunate Rear Admiral John Byng, sent in 1758 to relieve Minorca from the French with a poorly equipped squadron, was made a scapegoat for the failure of his mission and paid the price of his failure with his life. Acquitted at a court-martial of cowardice, he was nevertheless found guilty of neglect of duty and condemned to death. The court's recommendation for mercy was disregarded by George II and the Admiral was shot at Portsmouth. While Bevan was at Minorca, however, tranquillity reigned; no doubt he would have preferred to have been there two years earlier when Paget, at the head of the 28th, stormed Port Mahon.

The government had been considering how it could use its forces in the Mediterranean to best advantage in offensive operations. It was finally decided in October 1800 to send General Sir Ralph Abercromby to expel the French Army of the Orient, as it was known, from Egypt. The 66-year-old General was a distinguished and able solder much loved by his troops. As a young man he had studied law at Edinburgh and Leipzig. However, soldiering was his forte and, after doing well in the West Indies campaign, he was sent to command in Ireland, but his remonstrances against the policy of the government led to his removal. Then, in 1799, he led an inexperienced force against the French at Helder in Holland, where he learnt valuable lessons.

The 28th was to be part of Abercomby's expeditionary force and would serve in Major-General John Moore's brigade. Thus Bevan would be provided with his first taste of action against the French. The fleet of warships and transports left Malta towards the end of 1800 bound for the eastern Mediterranean. The first port of call was the sheltered bay of Marmaris on the Turkish mainland opposite Rhodes, where the expedition was to prepare for its operation and in particular to practise disembarkation and landings. These preparations and rehearsals, lasting seven weeks, had the support of the Turks who did not relish the presence of the French in Egypt, a country still, at least nominally, owing suzerainty to the Ottoman Empire. Indeed there was a Turkish army at Jaffa under the Grand Vizier, admittedly of mixed quality, waiting to move south against the French to avenge their recent heavy defeat at the hands of General Kléber at Heliopolis.

As Abercromby neared Egypt he was uneasy about the task given him on various grounds. For instance he was woefully short of horses and wagons, and, almost more important, he lacked intelligence about the strength and disposition of the French army. And there were no proper maps available. He would therefore be very short of information about the coast on which his men were to land. Above all, it would, with his great lumbering armada, be quite impossible to achieve surprise.

CHAPTER TWO

Egypt

When the invasion fleet reached Aboukir Bay, 14 miles or so east of Alexandria, it anchored some six or seven miles from the shore and waited for good weather. In the meantime Abercromby and Moore, on whose judgement the Commander-in-Chief placed much reliance, made a reconnaissance by launch of the target coastline to determine just where the troops should land.

The combined operation between the navy and the army began when a blue rocket was fired at 2 am on 8 March 1801 from Admiral Lord Keith's flagship *Foudroyant*. This was a signal for men to leave the troopships and, in the cases of some, the embraces of their wives and children, and transfer to the fleet of small boats. At 3 am a second rocket blazed across the sky and the seamen began to row for the distant shore. Moving in three separate and highly organized waves, with Bevan in the first of them, there were in all some 200 landing craft. These included 58 flat boats drawing only nine inches of water and loaded with 50 men, 37 launches each with 25 men and 84 rowboats with 10 men. The infantrymen sitting on the floorboards were heavily laden with three days' rations, two spare shirts and socks, blankets, entrenching tools, a canteen of water, 60 rounds of ammunition and two spare flints. Behind the first wave came rescue cutters with more troops towing launches with artillery pieces.[1] An assorted collection of gunboats accompanied the armada to give some kind of covering fire.

The assault force was around 5,500 strong. Reinforcements would come ashore later, giving Abercromby's task force a total

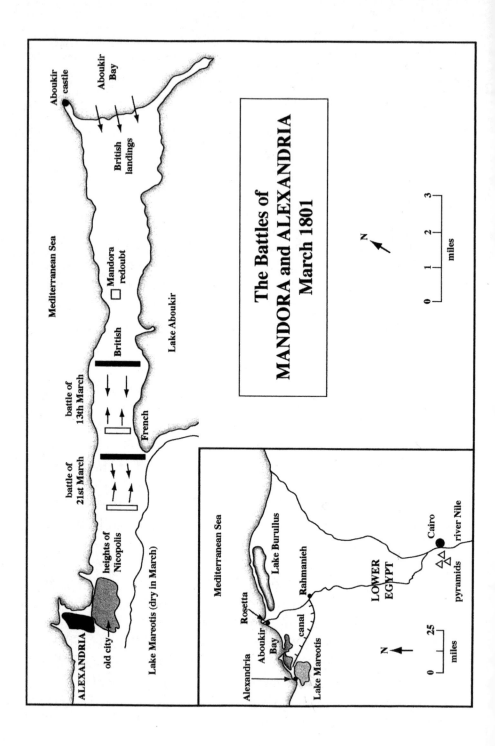

The Battles of
MANDORA and ALEXANDRIA
March 1801

strength of nearly 15,000. French troops in Egypt at the time numbered some 23,500 under their overall commander in Cairo, Jacques Menou, disposed at various locations. Menou, known as Abdullah on account of his conversion to Islam, had been slow to reinforce the Alexandria sector of his command. There the local commander, Louis Friant, thought that with his 2,000 infantry and cavalry he could defeat a British attack. Abercromby believed he was facing a much larger force.[2]

As daylight came the boats paused to get into exact order. Then some time after 8 am the seamen finally started pulling for the final spurt to the beach. In the lead barge, flying the flag of St George, were Captain Alexander Cochrane of the Royal Navy (later to be an Admiral), the officer in charge of the landings, and John Moore, commanding the Reserve (a perhaps misleading appellation for a leading formation). Not far away was Paget and his men. Bevan crouched in the assault boat, keeping a steady eye on his company commander. On shore enemy troops and guns had been seen moving into position in the sandhills and among the clumps of trees overlooking the beach.

As the boats came into range of the French artillery they were raked by roundshot and grape. There was also enfilading fire from the cannon at Aboukir Castle at the northern end of the beach. Soon the musket fire of the French infantry opened up. Except from the gunboats there could be no answering fire, but some of the invading force, in a spontaneous release of tension began to cheer lustily as the boats nearing the shore entered the danger zone. Inevitably some boats were hit and sunk, notably two full of Coldstream guardsmen. At length the leading boats grounded. The men leapt out and began racing up the beach. On the right Moore led the 23rd (the Royal Welch Fusiliers), the 28th under Paget and the 40th (2nd Somersetshire) towards a huge central sandhill which dominated the shoreline. The men scrambled up this feature, often on hands and knees in loose sand, and at last reached the top of the ridge. From this dominating position they began to fire on the enemy ahead.

In some places along the beach confused hand-to-hand fighting developed between invader and invaded, but gradually the invaders prevailed and the French, now outnumbered, were forced to retreat. Through dash and determination the British had won a bridgehead and their troops soon began pressing westwards beyond the dunes.

The storming of the beach at Aboukir Bay must have been a stirring sight with the men in their tall shakos and their red and blue uniforms, bayonets gleaming, and led by their officers with their swords drawn. What a baptism of fire for Charles Bevan! The scene duly caught the imagination of military artists and the walls of many a Mess in future years would be adorned with paintings of the famous landing.

Paget had been right when he had written home on the eve of the landings that there was 'a certain devil in this army and that will carry it through thick and thin'. With the sandhills to their rear, the 28th presently found themselves in a plain where they soon came to be held up by two French six pounders. Captain Fred Browne (one day to command the regiment) and his grenadier company charged the position with their bayonets and captured the guns and two ammunition wagons. In the process twenty-one Frenchmen fell.[3] This obstacle removed, Paget continued his advance inland, covering some two miles before halting at midday for a break when the men could enjoy their rations of cold boiled bacon and biscuit washed down with water from their canteens.

All that morning's work had, of course, been done by the infantry and, especially on the right and in the centre, by the Reserve Brigade. According to Moore's journal:

The want of cavalry and artillery . . . prevented us from pursuing further and destroying the enemy. They made good their retreat, though with considerable loss. Ours amounted to 600 killed and wounded, of which the Reserve lost 400.[4]

For their outstanding roles in the fighting that day both the 28th and the 42nd (the Black Watch) were singled out by the Commander-in-Chief – the only two regiments to be mentioned in the despatches sent home to London.[5]

The army's position was still somewhat precarious, particularly its lines of supply. The bridgehead achieved lay at the eastern end of a narrow isthmus of land, never more than a mile or so wide and bordered by the sea to the north and Lake Aboukir to the south, leading westwards via the Heights of Nicopolis to the city of Alexandria.

Within four days of the landings reinforcements from the troop-ships helped to consolidate the army's position and to bring it up to strength. On 12 March Abercromby ordered an advance in two columns, the head of each protected by units of the Reserve under Moore and Brigadier-General Hildebrand Oakes. The 28th were on the extreme right, close to the sea as the troops struggled through loose sand in undulating broken country interspersed with palm groves. After three or four miles Moore called a halt and went forward to observe. In front of him he saw a great body of enemy infantry seemingly preparing for action. By now the French had been reinforced and had some 4,500 men[6] in position across the isthmus, including first class cavalry and strong artillery.

Abercromby was not a man to waste time. Characteristically he decided that he would attack the French the next day and try and turn their position. The thirteenth of March dawned fine and rum was served before the army moved off towards the enemy at about 6.30 am, the 28th leading the column on the right flank. The French at once opened up with their artillery, a cannonade described by Moore in his journal as 'tremendous'. The British remained cool and resisted French counter-attacks. During a long day's fighting the enemy was pushed back in the direction of Nicopolis and as darkness fell the British attack was called off. In what came to be known as the Battle of Mandora (after a redoubt at the narrowest part of the isthmus) British losses had been heavy

– 1,300 men killed and wounded. The 28th lost two officers killed and Charles Bevan was severely wounded. Charles was, it seems, along with thirty or forty other men of the 28th, the victim of well-directed French round-shot ricocheting through the columns.[7] For him, therefore, after six exhilarating days, the fighting was over for the moment. Consequently he was not present when the main Battle of Alexandria was fought eight days later on 21 March some two miles to the west of the Mandora engagement site. This time the French, by now numbering 11,600, including 1,460 cavalry, attacked the numerically slightly superior British in a bid to destroy the invading force.[8] Here the 28th won fresh laurels, especially when, Paget having fallen seriously wounded in the neck with grapeshot, their acting Commanding Officer had given the order at a critical moment, 'Rear rank 28th! Right about face!'[9] Then the two ranks stood back to back to rebuff, successfully, the furious onslaught of a French cavalry charge. As a result of their action the 28th were granted the honour, unique among infantry regiments, of being entitled to wear the regimental badge at the back, as well as the front of their head-dress.

The British victory at Alexandria proved to be decisive, even though this was not at once apparent. But it was not without its cost: 1436 men had been killed or wounded. Among the fallen was Abercromby himself, fatally wounded in the thigh. Subsequently a peerage was conferred on his widow and the title, a barony, was afterwards enjoyed by his eldest son. Moore, Oakes, Paget and, of course, Bevan were among the many wounded. Some would, in due course, convalesce in the cool of Rosetta, on the Nile delta.

There was much for General Hutchinson, the new commander, to do. Menou had retired with his troops behind the strong defences protecting the city of Alexandria. There were, however, plenty of French troops in the delta and in Cairo. Hutchinson moved slowly – too slowly for some, including Paget – and methodically in his task of rounding up and expelling these forces from Egypt. First Colonel Brent Spencer, a gallant battalion commander, captured Rosetta in April. Then in May Hutchinson moved southwards with three brigades and some cavalry to the communications centre of Rahmanieh before proceeding towards Cairo. Nowhere was strong French resistance met. Also approaching Cairo from the north-east was the Grand Vizier and his ragged Turkish army, which, mainly motivated by the prospect of plunder, had come up surprisingly fast from Gaza.

The 28th and 42nd had remained behind with the containing force outside Alexandria under the tireless Major-General Eyre Coote who, it is said, never took his clothes off at night during the whole campaign. Now Hutchinson summoned these two seasoned regiments – the former still commanded by Paget, now recovered from his wound – to help in the investment of Cairo. But the 18-day march to the capital by the 28th proved to be unnecessary[10] because, in the event, the 10,000-strong French garrison capitulated, an armistice being signed on 28 June without a shot being fired. Afterwards the British commander organized visits to the great monuments for all ranks, the splendour of which greatly impressed one Sergeant Joseph Coates of the 28th.

After the fall of Cairo the 28th, with its strength down to 338 compared to 587 at the time of the landings, went back to Alexandria. The regiment again joined the Reserve under Moore and took up its station before the Heights of Nicopolis, ready at a moment's notice to assault the enemy. Coote for his part had kept the besiegers ever on the alert, the troops standing to every day an hour before daylight.[11]

As for Bevan we do not know how long he took to recover from his wound and so cannot be sure whether he went to Cairo and saw the Sphinx and the Pyramids. But after the return of the regiment to Alexandria, Captain George Gough, who commanded the Light Company, returned home to England, and his place was taken, as we do know, by Bevan.[12] This important post would certainly not have gone to him unless he had emerged from the warm work experienced by the Regiment in Egypt with credit and, in so doing, had gained the confidence of Paget.

By mid-August there was no real fight left in the French

garrison at Alexandria and at the end of the month Menou surrendered the city, which was finally entered by British troops on 2 September. With the campaign over the expeditionary force dispersed to England, Malta and the West Indies. The 28th, and Bevan with it, stayed behind in Egypt as part of the garrison of 6,000 kept there under General Moore.[13]

CHAPTER THREE

Plymouth, Fermoy and Folkestone

The 28th Foot, with Charles Bevan, left Egypt in the autumn of
1802, embarking on three naval frigates for the voyage home, and
duly arrived in Hillsea barracks, Portsmouth.[1] Within a week they
were off to Winchester and then on to Alresford and Alton in aid
of the civil authorities, the country still being plagued with bread
riots. But they were soon on the move again, this time to
Plymouth, where that summer the Regiment raised a second
battalion, numbering 1000 men. In a stirring welcome to the new
battalion, Colonel Sir Edward Paget, as he had now become, issued
an Order of the Day. In this he

> desires to impress on the minds of all young soldiers that they
> have the good fortune of being incorporated with a regiment
> that upwards of a century has been uninterruptedly employed
> in the acquirement of Honour and Reputation. He wishes
> them to know that they have, upon their right and left,
> comrades accustomed to victory who have often met with and
> know how to chastise that insolent, vain boasting enemy. . . .
> He wishes every individual at once to consider himself an old
> soldier.[2]

The enlargement of the Regiment came about just after the
renewal of hostilities between England and France. The Treaty of
Amiens, signed in March 1802, had provided only a temporary
lull – just 14 months – in the long saga of the Napoleonic

19

wars. The conflict had now taken a new turn with Napoleon preparing to invade Britain from northern France, where in camps outside Boulogne huge contingents of French soldiers began to concentrate.

One man especially imbued with the spirit of regimental and personal honour reflecting the ethos of the time was Charles Bevan. His conduct was always regulated by what he felt to be the highest standards of duty and integrity. This was certainly one reason why he had been selected to command the Light Company. Such a company in an infantry regiment had, in those days, a skirmishing and reconnaissance role. Moreover, a light company would be composed of the crack soldiers of the regiment. It was a feather in Bevan's cap to have been entrusted with this command and he had the good opinion of at least one senior NCO of the Regiment. Coates, mentioned before and now a sergeant-major, recounts how, as he was about to go on leave, he met Bevan in Exeter. Clearly Coates, as a long-serving NCO, was disappointed only to have received a month's leave after so many years' service overseas. At this chance meeting he applied to Bevan for an extension of leave and as a result got an extra month. Later Bevan was to express his regret on more than one occasion when Coates decided to leave the Regiment.

In October 1803 Paget was promoted to Brigadier-General, then a temporary rank, and sent to Fermoy, 15 miles north of Cork, to command a brigade in which both battalions of the 28th were to serve. Paget had recognized Bevan's ability and took him to Ireland as his brigade major. This was a post – in effect that of the principal staff officer to the brigade commander – much sought after by ambitious young officers. Sir William Gomm, who as a young man was with Wellington in the Peninsular War and was Commander-in-Chief in India in 1850, wrote of the post: 'The pay and rank are the same as an ADC. The officer has the rank of Major during the time he holds the employment and he is not considered as generally belonging to the General's family as the ADC. The situation is more independent'.[3]

Bevan was to serve in Fermoy for a little less than year. In the early 19th century Fermoy, though not a big place, was one of the barrack towns of Ireland with at least four separate barrack areas, two of them in the town itself, and a military cemetery. It is not surprising, therefore, that it was the site of a brigade headquarters. Paget did not live in the house provided in the barracks for the general. Instead he lived in a larger house – he once referred to it as a 'mansion' – where he could indulge his love of entertaining. Very probably, whatever Gomm said, Bevan was part of Paget's establishment. The Blackwater, a notable salmon river, flowed through the town and would have afforded recreation for any fisherman in a country which outside Dublin was regarded as a dull posting.

Before going to Fermoy an important event had occurred in Bevan's life. While at Plymouth he had met and fallen in love with Mary Dacres, the eldest daughter of Rear Admiral and Mrs Richard Dacres. The Admiral had a command in Plymouth at this time and was hoping for further preferment. His was a large and sociable family (two sons, both in the navy, and five daughters). From among the youth and beauty of local society Charles had chosen well, for Mary had personality and intelligence as well as notably good looks. The two were engaged by the spring of 1804 and the Admiral must have approved of his future son-in-law.

It was a love match and Charles would turn out to be an affectionate and devoted, if often absent, husband. We are fortunate that several of his early letters to Mary have survived. His impatience at their separation, and his fervour, is revealed in them. For instance in one dated 27 May 1804 written from Fermoy he regrets that he will not be able to see his beloved in the near future:

I am very anxious to compare your picture with yourself as on a more intimate acquaintance with it I begin to fancy it very like my dearest love!! I have a thousand things to say to you and places to propose which if realised!! but it is impossible to write on these subjects as I fear my imagination, perhaps too ardent, may lead me to hope what for your dear sake must not be I need hardly tell you what this is – Now, how can I ever again part with you, indeed I did not want the reality of absence, to convince me how painfully it is to be endured.[4]

It is clear from these early letters that an understanding and close relationship had quickly developed between the two young people. Charles obviously enjoyed giving Mary his thoughts and ideas on what he considered were serious or important subjects as well as, in lighter vein, passing on to her local regimental gossip and other news from Fermoy. Not surprising in one as ambitious as he, his plans for purchasing his majority were often at the fore-front of his mind, a matter which he constantly mentioned to Mary. Then he would muse, displaying a lively interest in current affairs, about how the war with France might develop; for instance, the possible need for British expeditions to the Spanish coast, a suggestion put forward with some prescience. Sometimes what he had to say revealed his mischievous sense of humour. For example, concerning the son of Mrs Dewes, the paymaster's wife, a report that he was a 'fine child' caused him to comment to Mary, 'I am sure it ought to be a large one if it bears any resemblance to either of its parents'. Then again it gave him much 'satisfaction', for some impish reason, that the lady spectators at the half-yearly inspec-tion of troops by General Eyre Coote

> were extremely well soaked by a repetition of heavy showers which I have but little doubt saved the washerwomen an infinity of trouble – for these ladies do not appear to consider cleanliness at all necessary to add to the lustre of their charms.[5]

Nor could he forebear from describing to Mary a dinner party he attended at which Lord Thanet, imprisoned some years before for riotous assembly, was present with his German wife who had for many years been his mistress. He reminded her too of the sentence imposed on Thanet, namely his right hand to be cut off, his property to be confiscated and 12 months imprisonment in the Tower. (Only the last part of the sentence was apparently carried out.)[6] His letters for the most part are well-expressed and often show a certain shrewdness about life and events. Always he treated Mary as an equal and as his confidant. On one matter they disagreed. Mary (alas, none of her letters to Charles have survived) believed that soldiers' wives should accompany their husbands abroad, while Charles thought they were better off at home.

Charles also showed a great interest in Mary's family and voiced his regrets that her father had not got the command he had hoped for. In fact Admiral Dacres would soon go to the West Indies, where he was on station in Jamaica in June 1805 with five ships of the line under his command. This was at the time when Nelson came flying across the Atlantic, chasing Admiral Villeneuve, only to hurry back home towards the end of the summer before setting out on his fateful voyage in *Victory* for the southern tip of Spain and final glory at Trafalgar. Charles had also become friendly with Barrington, the elder of Mary's two naval brothers, a man destined to die young of fever.

We begin quite soon to gain the impression that Charles was more at home with Mary's family than with his own. He did not seem to have a close relationship with his mother, who gives the impression from Charles's letters of not really being interested in her son, his career and later his family. He was disappointed that she was not going to be able to give the young couple any financial help when they got married, although there may well have been perfectly good reasons for this, unrecorded by Charles in his letters. Then he expressed surprise to Mary, almost complainingly, that his mother was going to remain in London during the summer rather than travel to the country. 'It is very strange to me,' he writes, 'that people who might live in the country with <u>every</u> necessary comfort should prefer a <u>street</u> – but if they are happy it is certainly sufficient.' (Bevan's emphasis)[7]

Paget returned to England in June 1804, just after Napoleon had had himself proclaimed Emperor of the French, to be given command of a brigade of militia at Colchester. Bevan went with him, still his brigade major, and then followed him to the Kentish coast outside Folkestone. Here Paget's brigade was stationed next door to Major-General Moore's famous experimental brigade, about which something must be said because of the brigade's influence on developments in the army and therefore on Bevan's own approach to his profession.

Moore, a highly gifted and enlightened man, had had wide campaigning experience and, as we have seen, done well in Egypt. The son of a distinguished Scottish doctor, he had been educated in Glasgow, was fluent in French and Italian and a lover of books and poetry. Somehow he also found time to be an MP for five years. In 1803 he had been appointed to command a brigade at Shorncliffe training camp near Folkestone with the object of providing the army with a corps of light infantry. Emphasis in the training was placed on marksmanship, on how to patrol, how to undertake duty in outposts and perform the role of rear and advance guards. Above all, merit and good conduct were to be rewarded. Moore was also something of a fitness fanatic and wanted to obtain the right quality of young officer for his new cadres. All his officers were encouraged to get to know their NCOs and men. In matters of discipline he could be tough, but he was keen at the same time to avoid the indiscriminate flogging of soldiers. He was highly successful in his endeavours at Shorncliffe and the troops he was responsible for training became the nucleus of the Light Division which later did so well in the Peninsular War. Moore and Paget, in many ways model soldiers, were both admired by Bevan, the aspiring young officer. This speaks well of Bevan's judgment of his seniors.

As the troops were trained at Folkestone, few could be unaware of the threat posed by the tens of thousands of French soldiers who had congregated on the other side of the Straits of Dover and of their plans to invade England. On arrival in Kent Bevan was telling Mary about this and of the:

An example of CB's handwriting from a letter to Mary written from near Folkestone in November 1804.

very threatening appearance that the Boulogne flotilla at present assumes – the relative situation of this Brigade which is with the exception of General Moore's the nearest to the coast – we hear a constant and heavy cannonade. I am also informed that on a very clear day it is possible to distinguish, from a signal post about two miles from our quarters, the French lines of encampment.[8]

The effect of this threat, he told her, was that he was unable to obtain leave of absence to go down to Plymouth to see her. The continued separation from his fiancée constantly frustrated Charles, who wondered when times might change.

When, when will that happy period arrive? I assure you the dread of its distance affords no addition to the very moderate share of good spirits I at present possess, neither does the contemplation of difficulties which are alas! too conspicuous in our path to happiness by any means tend to dissipate afflictions which at present must assume but a melancholy hue. I, however, strive and will resolutely strive to contemplate the fairer side of this constantly thought on subject – and now, Mary, I think I shall have your permission to be a little gloomy.[9]

These thoughts reflected a deeply pessimistic side to Charles' character about which we will hear more.

Nevertheless, during his months near Folkestone progress was being steadily made in the two goals closest to his heart, namely his marriage to Mary and the purchasing of his majority. The former, of course, depended on the latter, for we may suppose that Admiral Dacres had laid down as a condition to giving his consent to the marriage that Bevan's promotion to major be gazetted. Purchase in the army was never straightforward. The minimum price for all commissions was fixed by Royal Warrant, though a commission could be traded for a higher price when the agreed non-regulation premium went to the seller. The Crown at the same time retained the right of selecting and approving an officer's successor.[10] The process of purchase could be a long-drawn-out one.

Eventually Bevan's negotiations with Major Groves of the 28th came to a successful conclusion, and by the end of November he had purchased his majority for the sum of 3,000 guineas. This sounds a huge sum but it was the going rate at the time. George Scovell, who became distinguished in the Napoleonic Wars as Wellington's code-breaker of French military correspondence, paid £3,150 in 1803 to buy a captaincy in the Dragoons.[11] Bevan at last could write to Mary on 11 November to say that he cherished the hope that he would 'very very soon [be] calling you mine' and, rather charmingly, telling her

> not to forget to enclose the size of your finger by means of a piece of silk or something of that nature, that I may be the happy bearer of the ring which is to make you my prisoner for ever.[12]

CHAPTER FOUR

Bremen, Copenhagen and Gothenburg

Undoubtedly the most important event in the first year of the Bevans' marriage occurred on 7 November 1805 when Mary gave birth to a son, christened Charles. But her husband, Charles, was away from home for Mary's confinement.

When Charles resumed regimental duties after his time as Paget's brigade major was up he took his bride to Fermoy in Ireland where both battalions of the 28th were still stationed. In the spring of 1805 the regiment moved to Birr in County Offaly, and then in August were encamped for a time at the Curragh, 20 miles south-west of Dublin, before the two battalions were separated, the first going to Mallow and the second to Dublin.[1] We do not know whether Mary, expecting her baby in November, was for ever traipsing around Ireland after her husband. Probably not. Also it is likely that to have the baby she went home to Plymouth to be with her mother. What is, however, certain is that in October the first battalion of the 28th, especially asked for by Lord Cathcart for his expedition to North Germany, embarked at Cork for Bremen. So Bevan parted from his wife and was off to the wars again.

This expedition had come about following the establishment in the summer of 1804 of a coalition against Napoleon, inspired by the Prime Minister, William Pitt, between Britain, Austria, Russia, Sweden and Naples. For two years Napoleon had been preparing to invade Britain, and for this purpose, as we have seen, had gathered together an army of over 200,000 men on the channel coast. But, mainly on account of British naval supremacy, this invasion never took place, and instead Napoleon had turned his attention to central Europe, where he proceeded to gain a sequence of startling victories. Faster than his opponents had anticipated, he marched his armies away from their encampments outside Boulogne and down to the Danube in Bavaria. Here he compelled the Austrians to surrender at Ulm on 20 October 1805. Six weeks later at Austerlitz near Brno (now in the Czech Republic) he smashed the Austrians and Russians, forcing the former to sign an armistice and the latter to return home.

The following year it was the turn of the Prussians to receive hammer blows from the French, who beat them decisively at the battles of Jena and Auerstadt. Undisputedly, Napoleon had made himself master of most of continental Europe.

But we must return to the autumn of 1805 before Napoleon's victories over the Austrians. The British government decided at this time to send an expedition, initially of about 11,000 men, to North Germany, using Hanover as its base. The plan was to expel the small French force of 4,000 from the Electorate and then recover Holland with help from Russia, Sweden and above all Prussia. The last-named country might even be induced, so it was thought, to declare war on France.

Bevan and his regiment, at almost full strength with 968 men, had a rough passage across the North Sea, two transports in the fleet foundering, one with the headquarters of the 26th (the Cameronians) on board. Once in Germany the 28th were in due course brigaded, under Paget, with the 23rd, the 4th Foot (King's Own) and some of the 95th (The Rifle Brigade).[2] At first Bevan and the 28th found themselves billeted at Blumental on the Weser just north of Bremen (which was to be the right of a British line extending to Verden on its left). Then, early in the new year, they moved to the suburbs of Bremen, by which time Lord Cathcart, the British commander, had, following the arrival of reinforcements, about 26,000 troops under him. But now their allies let the British down. The Prussians, on whom much depended, proved unreliable and came to an accommodation with the French. This development affected the Swedes, who also had second thoughts about the coalition. Thus, with the ground cut from under their feet and especially as a result of the defeats suffered by the Austrians in the south, the British found themselves isolated. Consequently Cathcart and his force, with nothing achieved and further disheartened by the news of the death from disease and overwork of the 46-year-old William Pitt, had no alternative but to withdraw from the continent.

The troops, therefore, re-embarked at Cuxhaven. Bevan, disappointed not to have seen any action – the regimental records report 'they remained for 6 weeks in a state of inactivity'[3] – had at least the consolation of returning home at the end of February 1806 to see his son for the first time. The Regiment had now left Ireland and, on disembarking at Yarmouth, they were due for a lengthy spell in East Anglia. First they marched to Woodbridge and then on to Colchester, which would become their base. Until the French revolutionary wars troops had been badly housed when they were not on the move. They usually had to make do with ad hoc quarters and billets, or, for training purposes, tented camps. Then, in 1793, came a major barrack-building programme which began to provide much better facilities. At Colchester the 28th, at least for some of the time they were there, occupied cavalry barracks.

The Bevans remained in Essex for 15 months during which time a second son, Thomas, was born. Mention should here be made of two people who played a significant part in their lives. One was a widow, Mrs Shaw, a cousin on Charles' side. She took a keen interest in his career and marriage, and both Charles and Mary wrote regularly to her. She was well liked and respected by the Bevans, who took pains to give her all their news, and one cannot help speculating as to whether she did not help over the money needed by Charles to purchase his promotions. Certainly she was generous to the young couple and a story has been handed down through the family that she lent her country house, between

Newbury and Hungerford, to the Bevans for their honeymoon. This house was eventually left by Mrs Shaw in her will to Charles and Mary's children.

The other person was Charles Paterson, known as Jim, a fellow officer in the 28th and a close friend of Charles. Some years later Paterson would marry Mary's sister, Eleanor. Paterson was a Scot who did well in the Peninsular War, becoming a brevet Lieutenant-Colonel, only to fall, mortally wounded, at Vitoria, the last great battle in Spain in that war. William Keep of the 28th wrote of how Paterson's presence in the battalion 'affords us with much satisfaction and I am indebted to him for numerous kindnesses'. As for Eleanor, Keep, after commenting on her 'most interesting condition' as Paterson left for Spain, said she might have been described as

the Hebe of Devonshire . . . She is a most charming woman and he must feel his separation from her very acutely at this period particularly.[4]

We have not so far given any physical description of Charles Bevan. There is little to go on except for the miniature of him in oils which has been handed down through the family. He is in the uniform of the 28th and was probably a captain at the time the painting was done. Perhaps it was undertaken just before his marriage. He appears with large eyes, prominent nose and small mouth. His shoulders are narrow, though this may be caused by the artist having insufficient space to work within a miniature. The general impression is of a slightly effeminate-looking man; there is no evidence there of a tough, rude soldier. There is a hint that he was intelligent, also that he could have been both fastidious and obstinate. As for his physique, the scanty evidence we have suggests he was of average height and medium build.

In the summer of 1807 overseas service for the 28th was again in the wind and Bevan found himself, towards the end of June, writing from the village of Danbury, outside Chelmsford, to his wife, who was at that time staying with her parents at Burlesdon near Southampton. At Danbury he was camped with 300 men on an attractive common living in a 'marquee . . . a most comfortable habitation'. Sounding cheerful, his letter was full of regimental doings and also of news from his mother and sister Julia, writing no less than three letters to Mary in just seven days. He hoped that she had not neglected her cough and said he missed her 'very much indeed and my poor little Charles is becoming so good a playfellow that I daily regret that he and I can not run around together'. He was clearly annoyed at the 'scandalous charge' for a bill of 'nearly four pounds for damages due to the Quarters we occupied in the Cavalry barracks'. He thought that, despite his efforts at resisting the charge, he would have to pay up since they had occupied the quarters on favourable terms. He makes mention of his commanding officer, Colonel Johnson, whose small children are compared unfavourably to his own and to 'farmer' Dewes, the paymaster.[5] He had found Major Ibbotson 'just as much of an old woman as ever, but very good natured and very gentlemanlike therefore pleasant'. Bevan mentioned these people, and others along the way, as they were all well known to Mary and there was nothing she liked more than to receive some regimental gossip.

Interestingly for us, and no doubt for Mary, Bevan includes in one letter a description of his day:

The history of my life at present is easily told – get up about Eight, Breakfast, dressing then fills up the time till Parade; then an excursion till about two or three – then rest till dinner – after dinner Parade; and after that go to bed as soon as I can. Generally about half past nine or ten. Sometimes play a game at cricket but these mornings drills have put a stop to that, which I am not sorry for as it is almost too hot for such violent exercise. The Mess now consists of nearly 30. You may suppose not the pleasanter for being so numerous.[6]

Bevan was always highly susceptible to changes in climate and his letters are liberally sprinkled with references to temperature, sun and rain. He was right about the extreme heat in June, for the summer of 1807 was famous for its blisteringly hot weather and there were many cases of farm workers fainting in the hayfields of Buckinghamshire.

As for their destination, Bevan was in the dark as much as anyone else, except that he 'knew' it would be a continental one and that they would probably be serving again under Lord Cathcart. Bevan was right on both counts and in a month or so he would be joining a transport bound for Denmark.

Cathcart had in fact received his orders in June and would be landing on the island of Rügen in the Baltic on 16 July with the advance guard of a force promised to the Russians and Prussians as some kind of joint diversion with the Swedes against Napoleon. But once again decisions made in London had been overtaken by events on the continent. News of the defeat of the Russians on 14 July by Napoleon at the Battle of Friedland did not reach London until the end of the month. Next, moving with his usual rapidity, Napoleon met the impressionable young Czar, Alexander I, on that famous raft on the River Niemen and concluded on 7 July the important Treaty of Tilsit. Alexander, won over by the French Emperor and his personality, recognized all of Napoleon's conquests and, moreover, undertook to join him in an alliance against Britain, whose ships were already being excluded from Europe and its ports under the Emperor's continental blockade.

The Foreign Secretary, George Canning, had learnt some of the secret provisions of Tilsit, in particular Napoleon's plan to obtain control over the remaining neutral fleets in Europe. The British government at once made contact with Denmark, seeking to persuade that country to place her fleet in British hands until the end of the war. The Danes rejected this proposal with some indignation. Acting, therefore, with commendable speed, indeed taking a leaf out of Napoleon's ruthless book, the British government assembled a fleet, with transports bearing 18,000 men, at

Yarmouth and directed Admiral James Gambier to sail to Denmark, where he would be joined by Cathcart and his men who were to be withdrawn from Rügen. The fleet duly arrived off Elsinore Roads. The two commanders made a curious pair: Gambier, a vigorous man known for his extreme evangelical views, had a habit of distributing religious tracts among the lower deck, while Cathcart was a somewhat timid commander in the field, though, as if making amends for this, he had sound political sense.

The landings, unopposed, were made at Vedbeck, eight miles north of Copenhagen, on 16 August. Bevan found that his regiment was brigaded with the Guards and the 79th (Cameron Highlanders) in the 1st Division. Initially they occupied ground northwards towards Frederiksborg, where there was a royal palace. On one occasion the Guards, followed by the band of the 28th, had just reached the road to the north from Copenhagen when some members of the royal family were seen coming from the capital in a carriage. At once becoming aware of the royal presence, the Guards wheeled into line, opened ranks and presented arms, while the band of the 28th broke into 'God Save the King'![7] The astonished feelings of the travellers (they were two princesses, nieces of the King) can, with some difficulty, be imagined. What on earth could it mean when a hostile army on its way to besiege your capital city behaved in this fashion?

The army, meeting only limited resistance, soon surrounded most of Copenhagen. In the only battle of the campaign Sir Arthur Wellesley, with the Reserve, routed the Danish militia forces trying to relieve the city at Køge. On another occasion a foray from the capital was made by a force of 2000 Danes supported by artillery but they were soon driven back through the gates. A difficulty for the Danes was that their army in Jutland was prevented by the Royal Navy from crossing the sea to Zealand to help the defenders of Copenhagen.

Cathcart found attacking the friendly Danish people distasteful and hoped they would quickly surrender. Consequently he delayed opening fire with his guns on the city, but, as the besieged did not at once oblige him, his bombardment began on 2 September with forty mortars, ten howitzers, thirty cannon and some rockets, which were being used in action for the first time. This cannonade continued for four days and on 7 September the city, which had suffered much damage, capitulated. A flank battalion formed of the grenadiers from several regiments under the command of Major Browne of the 28th (we have met this intrepid officer before) took peaceful possession of the citadel and the dockyard.

The real objective of the expedition, the Danish fleet, was lying in the dockyard trapped by the Royal Navy. Altogether fifteen ships of the line and thirty smaller vessels to the value of £4,500,000[8] fell into the hands of the British. The Danish fleet, with men of the 28th helping to man two prize ships (one of 84 guns and the other of 74), were sailed back to England in October. Finally, Lieutenant-Colonel J. Wynch, who makes his first appearance in this story, was appointed Lieutenant-Governor of Copenhagen.[9]

At a cost of 200 casualties, the expedition, an audacious one, regarded by the opposition and some others in parliament as high-handed, had achieved its aim quickly and efficiently. This was in marked contrast to the previous continental expedition in which Bevan had served. There is perhaps a temptation to think that the pushy Bevan somehow managed to get for himself in Denmark a share of the little action there was, but there is no evidence that this was so. More likely, his part in the expedition was a disappointingly passive one. Mary, at least, would have been relieved when the 28th landed in Portsmouth in November and marched back to Colchester to reoccupy their old barracks.

In dogged vein, Britain, now friendless in Europe with the exception of Sweden and Portugal, continued to try and frustrate Napoleon as best she could. King Gustavus IV of Sweden hated Napoleon and refused to close his Baltic ports in accordance with the Emperor's demands. Punitive action followed when, without any declaration of war, Russia, ally of France, suddenly invaded Swedish Finland, while Prussia and Denmark both formally declared war on Sweden. This gave rise in Britain to the fear that France itself might invade Sweden from Denmark. It was in these circumstances that the British decided to send an expedition to Sweden under Sir John Moore, recently returned home from duty in Sicily, to aid the Swedes in operations against the French. Unfortunately, the government did not define the object of the expedition sufficiently clearly; at least that is what Moore, with some justification, confided to his mother.[10]

The 28th, brigaded this time with the 4th and said to be composed mostly of young Irishmen,[11] received their orders at Colchester in April 1808 to march to Harwich, where they were to embark for Gothenburg. Bevan, who had had some five months at home with Mary and his sons, went with them. Once again, and to his delight, he found himself soldiering with Edward Paget, who this time was his divisional commander. Paget had married soon after Bevan and, sadly, in 1806 had lost his wife in childbirth. It is said he was so grief-stricken that he at once volunteered for service overseas, and so found himself in Sicily with Moore.

The fleet assembled at Yarmouth and, setting sail on 10 May, reached its destination seven days later, anchoring off the Swedish coast. There the hapless soldiers, numbering 11,000, half of them Germans, were destined to stay bottled up on their small transports for many idle weeks without knowing the reasons for this state of affairs.

Moore faced two special difficulites on arrival in Sweden. One was his precise objectives. The other, a huge one, was Gustavus. The highly autocratic King, aged 30, was an unbalanced man of excitable temperament. Some said that he was mad. As a start the British troops were forbidden to land in Sweden. The problem was that Gustavus and the British government had different ideas as to what use the troops should be put. The King did not wish to use them defensively. On the contrary, he wished to employ them, under his own personal command, to attack Norway and Denmark; later he even suggested Russia as a target. All this was not in accordance with the woolly instructions given to Moore by

Lord Castlereagh, Secretary for War. So Moore was obliged to refer back to his political master. In the event Castlereagh modified his orders to Moore, who would be entitled *in extremis* to withdraw his corps. There was no alternative for Moore but to go from Gothenburg to Stockholm, a journey which would take at least 60 hours, to beard the King in his palace. At first Gustavus seemed well disposed to his visitor, but when Moore, firm yet courteous, did not mince his words about the objects of the expedition, the King lost his temper. He as good as told Moore that he could not leave Stockholm without his, the King's, permission; in other words Moore was under house arrest.

Meanwhile the troops got through their days as best they could. Life, in fact, could not have been too disagreeable for them. Some of the soldiers had their wives and children with them. The weather was ideal and the troops were able to exchange their rations of salt pork or beef for fish. Forty or fifty lobsters could be bought for one dollar. The Swedes on shore were friendly and came in little boats to listen to the bands of the different regiments.[12] The men took it in turns to land on a nearby island for exercise and bathing. Regimental sports were organized. The young and dashing Harry Smith of the 95th won the long jump with a massive leap of 19 feet 4 inches.[13] Smith, four years later, would become famous when he married, on campaign in the Peninsular War, a lovely high-born Spanish girl of 14 plucked from the ruins of Badajoz. Still later, when he was Governor of the Cape, the town of Ladysmith was named after his wife. We do not know if Bevan took part in the sports. Probably not. He does not mention them in two surviving letters he wrote to Mary from Gothenburg. Certainly there is no evidence anywhere that he was any kind of sportsman. In fact he had been ill off Gothenburg with, so it sounds from what he told his wife, some sort of bilious attack or stomach upset. At any rate he was sent off by Paget, with the general's ADC for company, to see a famous lake and waterfall.

The two were away for a good three days, apparently travelling 180 miles. Bevan, deriving 'very much gratification' from his 'excursion', found the country 'in parts most beautiful', but had no comment to offer about the people or villages encountered on his journey. Bevan was undoubtedly lucky in being allowed this jaunt. It looks as if Paget had not forgotten the loyal service given him by his former brigade major.

In his letters to Mary Charles had plenty to say about their domestic affairs, always highly important to him. For instance, writing from shipboard off Gothenburg, he was 'mortified' that Mary, who was then staying in Campden, had not seen his mother, whom he described as being guilty of 'inattention to use the mildest word', to her daughter-in-law. He added the fierce rider that he 'would be attentive to no person upon earth who is otherwise to you'.[15] It was not as if his mother was far away from her daughter-in-law, as she too was 'in town'. Unhappily, this lack of apparent interest by his mother in Mary and in her grandchildren is a recurring theme in Bevan's letters. As if in contrast to his feelings for his own family, Charles seemed devoted to the Dacres, especially to Mary's mother.

Charles liked to tell Mary about happenings in the regiment, but he did not mention the unhappy accident which befell Brevet Major Dudingstone. Walking the deck one day, he glanced up and saw two boys of the Regiment up aloft clinging to the masthead. This tomfoolery was too much for the poor major. Yelling to them to come down, the Major burst a blood vessel, from which, invalided home, he subsequently died.[16]

Events in Stockholm were now moving to a climax. John Moore had no intention of being deprived of his liberty through the behaviour of a monarch he considered insane He decided, therefore, to make his 'escape'. This he did by disguising himself in the clothes – evidently previously acquired in case of need – of a peasant woman, and then slipping quietly away from the city. It is said that when he reached Gothenburg he managed, still in disguise, to board the British flagship without being challenged. Unrecognized by the Captain and his own staff, there was much hilarity when he threw off his skirt and bonnet and revealed himself. There was now no point in prolonging the expedition's stay in Swedish waters and the fleet sailed home, arriving at Spithead in the middle of July.

However much Bevan was looking forward to being reunited with Mary and the boys, he was to be disappointed. The government had other plans for Moore and his force. No disembarkation was allowed and once more the transports were on the move. This time their destination was Portugal. Before the ships left Portsmouth there was just time for new army orders to be put into effect. For some time hair powder had been abolished in the army. Then in 1804 pigtails, or queues as they were also known, were shortened to seven inches. Now, with the issue of a further set of regulations, army barbers boarded the ships and docked what was left of the men's pigtails. There followed a joyous ceremony when a colossal pile of queues were, with great relief and a lusty three cheers, tossed overboard into the keeping of Neptune!

CHAPTER FIVE

From Lisbon to Sahagun

The historian George Trevelyan has stated

> Napoleon's endeavour to enforce his 'continental system' for
> excluding British goods from Europe . . . drew him into the
> two most fatal errors of his career, the attempt to annex Spain
> against the will of its people and the invasion of the vastness
> of Russia.[1]

The sequence of events which led in 1808 to the British government sending troops to Portugal so as to help Spain in her
emerging struggle against France may be said to have begun in
October the previous year when Napoleon compelled Spain to sign
the secret Treaty of Fontainebleau. Under this Spain agreed to join
in an attack on Portugal, a county which had incurred Napoleon's
wrath by keeping its ports open to British ships and trade. Thus
was the way open for General Junot to march rapidly across Spain
and enter Lisbon with his troops at the end of November 1807,
just too late, however, to catch the Portuguese fleet shepherded
away by the Royal Navy in the nick of time. But Napoleon had
further plans. Under the pretence of helping Junot, he flooded
Spain with French troops.

The Spanish Royal family, distracted by domestic quarrels, was
then in crisis. King Charles IV, frightened at the turn of events,
decided to flee with his wife, Queen Maria Luisa, and her lover,
the sinister chief minister, Manuel Godoy, to South America. In

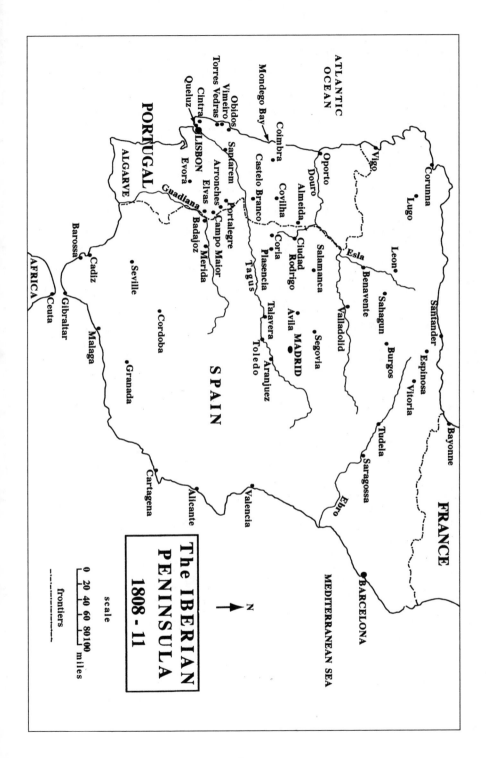

March 1808 the mob learnt about this at Aranjuez, where the Royal family had a palace, and rioted. In Madrid the hated Godoy's house was sacked and his life threatened. The terrified Charles now abdicated in favour of his degenerate son Ferdinand. Almost at once Marshal Joachim Murat, the innkeeper's son who would soon become King of the Two Sicilies, assumed command of all French troops in Spain and arrived in Madrid at the head of a corps.

Subsequently Ferdinand was, so it is said, decoyed by Napoleon to Bayonne. There both Charles and his son were induced by the French Emperor to renounce their rights to the Spanish crown. The now vacant throne was offered to and accepted by Napoleon's compliant eldest brother Joseph Bonaparte, the King of Naples. But, in laying and carrying out his plans, Napoleon had failed to take account of Spanish patriotism and, strangely, affection for Ferdinand. When the mob in Madrid discovered in May how they had been deceived they rose and killed in cold blood any French soldier they could lay their hands on. Although the disorders were ruthlessly suppressed – witness Goya's striking painting in the Prado *A military execution in 1808* – the flame of insurrection was now alight all over Spain, with revolutionary juntas springing up throughout the provinces. At the same time the spirit of rebellion spread to Portugal. In early June two delegates from the Asturias junta in northern Spain arrived in Falmouth to seek British aid against France, seen now as the common enemy. It did not take the British government long to forget its former state of war with Spain and to offer that country assistance. Happily, there were troops available: 9,500 men under Wellesley lying off Cork destined for, of all places, Venezuela; Moore's 10,000 troops about to return from Sweden, another 5,000 under Brent Spencer in troopships at Gibraltar and 3,000 under Beresford at Madeira.[2] The Cabinet, therefore, decided on 30 June to put together an expeditionary force composed of these separate elements and despatch it to Portugal.

Suddenly, in the summer of 1808, everything seemed to be happening at once in and around the Iberian landmass. Madrid had been reoccupied by General Castaños; there were risings against the French in Oporto and the Algarve, and British troops were now converging on Portugal from all directions. At last, so Bevan must have felt while ploughing through the Bay of Biscay in his cramped transport, a long period of inactivity was over and he would again be getting to grips with the French.

The first British troops ashore in Portugal were Wellesley's corps who landed uncomfortably among the breakers at Mondego Bay in the first week of August. Wellesley, charged with moving towards Lisbon 100 miles away, at once led his men to the south by way of Obidos, a village with pretty white-washed houses perched on a hillside, and Rolica, where he fought a brisk action against Junot's subordinate Laborde. A few days later Junot himself, anxious to throw the British back into the sea before they could be reinforced, attacked a strong British position carefully selected by Wellesley on a reverse slope at Vimeiro. The riflemen, trained by Moore, brought to bear a withering fire and all along the front the overconfident attacks by the enemy were smashed and Junot forced to retreat. The British were now admirably placed to turn their success in the field into a rout of the French forces. Unhappily military ineptitude intervened.

Back in London the army was determined to have old-stagers as its commanding generals in Portugal. Just arrived in his frigate offshore was Lt-Gen Sir Harry Burrard; he had been appointed second-in-command to the overall commander, the blimpish and absent Sir Hew Dalrymple, the Governor of Gibraltar. Famously, Wellesley proposed to Burrard, for a fleeting instance in command of the troops ashore, that the defeated French should be vigorously pursued to Lisbon. The cautious Burrard, to Wellesley's exasperation, said no and that they had better wait for Moore's troops, expected shortly. The next day Dalrymple, extraordinarily enough the army's third commander in 24 hours, appeared on the scene and confirmed this order. As if this missed opportunity was not enough, the British were now tactically outwitted by Junot who proposed under a flag of truce that the French army should be evacuated from Portugal. Dalrymple, without referring back to London, agreed to this and there followed the much criticized Convention of Cintra, to which on 31 August he, Burrard and, rashly, Wellesley (he did not read the final text) put their signatures. Under it the French army was allowed to be evacuated back to France on British ships with its equipment intact and various 'property' on board. The French soldiers would then be free to reenter the war. Unbelievably, 'property' included French loot such as melted-down church plate. The outcry in London about the Convention, when it was published in the *London Gazette* in mid-September, was so fierce that Dalrymple and Burrard were summoned home to face a court of inquiry. Wellesley, disgusted with the turn of events, had already left Portugal, but he too was required to face the music.

And what of Moore, the 28th and Bevan all this time? Moore's men had begun landing at Maceira Bay, not far from Vimeiro, on 25 August, that is four days after the battle there. These landings, as were Wellesley's, were unopposed, the main French forces being to the south. In intense heat the 28th began to march down to Lisbon. The men, having been on board ship so long, were sadly out of training, 'scarcely having the use of their limbs' in the words of one officer. At last they reached Queluz outside Lisbon where the army was now encamped for some weeks. In the capital, soldiers of the opposing armies were to be seen drinking and carousing together on the friendliest terms.[3] The responsibly married and sometimes rather anti-social Bevan did not, as far as we are aware, go to the excellent opera, which was frequented by both British and French officers, or explore the social life of Lisbon.

In the meantime Moore, to the evident satisfaction of Bevan, was appointed Commander-in-Chief of the British forces in Portugal, so ending the strange episode of musical chairs for the top army job with the expeditionary force. Moore was surprised at his appointment, for he thought he was out of favour politically and so had missed the bus for this command. The despatch appointing him to the post, signed on 26 September by the King and Castlereagh, enjoined him to employ the 30,000 infantry and 5000 cavalry entrusted to him in cooperating with the Spanish armies in the expulsion of the French from Spain.[4]

In the six weeks that Charles Bevan was at Queluz just three letters of his to Mary have survived. In them some gentle humour and quiet grumbling indicates the closeness of the relationship between husband and wife. For instance, concerning Mary's letters to him, Charles had a dig that the last one

> did not afford me any news but your letters always afford me the highest pleasure whether old or new; I have not yet got the long one which you tell me is to be very uninteresting – I have not hitherto found your correspondence so. I therefore am very anxious to see this letter which is to be of so very different a nature from the others.[5]

He complained too about the heat and the fact that he could not 'entirely get the better of my bilious afflictions'.

As usual he had a go at his frustrations at not getting promoted. He worried at the subject like a dog with a bone. Several majors, he wrote, younger than he had got promoted. If he did not get 'it' speedily, promotion would be of no use and he would not wish to have it. Then, in a fit of pessismism, he asserted he had practically given up all hope of being promoted. This was hard, he lamented, with more than a touch of self-pity, but he was 'pretty well accustomed to disappointments and what is more there is no relief'. On a similar tack he opined that 'rank is the thing' and he did not want to 'come home without a Lieutenant-Colonelcy'. On yet another he found when 'it' did arrive it would be in 'some dreadful corps'. No wonder, in such a bitter mood, he ended his letter 'Thirty years old and alas still a Major.'[6] At least he had let off steam, though this might have been at Mary's expense, something perhaps he did not consider.

He also commented on the accounts in the English newspapers

about the 'conduct' of Sir Hew Dalrymple, referring to the criticism the General had been subjected to regarding the Convention
of Cintra. Bevan evidently came to regard what Dalrymple had
done as dishonourable. Indeed he was, in the following year, to tell
Mary's naval brother, James, who has an important role in our
story much later on, that 'Sir Hew, if he had a military feeling
would have shot himself'. This was no doubt rather an absurd line
to take, but demonstrates how important military honour was to
Bevan.

Bevan had little to say to Mary about the land in which he found
himself or its people (though this may have been said in other non-
surviving letters), except to venture that Portugal was a 'miserable'
country. He was, however, pleased to acquire 'a very good mule'
which would be essential for the campaigning which lay ahead.
With his penchant for odd regimental gossip, he clearly enjoyed
making some pithy comments on a Grand Ball he had, perhaps
exceptionally, attended:

> [This was] given by the English Army to the Portuguese
> Nobility etc. It was as stupid as need be, I did not stay there
> long but poor little Dewes [the paymaster] who could not
> resist the temptations of a very elegant supper has been
> unwell ever since. You must not say a word about this but I
> thought it would amuse you. I do not know what we are to
> pay for this Ball but I fear much more than I think any Ball
> can be worth.[7]

These letters are full of references to Charles's immediate family
and for the first time we hear about Edward, his third son, born in
the early part of the year. He makes occasional reference to his
mother and to his sisters, Caroline and Julia. Caroline had written
him a letter, clearly a somewhat unusual event, but one which
caused him 'very great satisfaction'. He also promised to write to
Mary's father, the old Admiral, whose health had been damaged

probably beyond repair by the climate in the West Indies where he had just finished four years' service. Admiral Dacres was about to take a cure at Cheltenham Spa, as was General Spencer, due to leave Lisbon at any minute. Bevan hoped Spencer would carry home the letter he had just written to Mary as well as some pretty 'little trinkets' Charles was to obtain for her. Something went wrong unfortunately and Bevan never made the purchase. It is interesting that Bevan – after all he was only a major – had a sufficiently good relationship with the senior Spencer to ask him to carry his mail, or did it show Bevan to be just pushy?

Moore lost little time in getting his army on the road to Spain. Before the advance began he inspected the 28th, which was now at full strength, with '1100 bayonets' (the average full strength of an infantry battalion in those days would be some 980 officers and men in eight companies). The Regiment, brigaded with the 4th and 42nd, was in Major-General Alexander Fraser's division and was commanded by the redoubtable Major Fred Browne, an eccentric as well as a gallant officer. (At the end of the campaign, before embarking at Corunna, he traded his horse, which he was required by orders to shoot, for a pig. Alas, barter was to no avail. Pig and Browne got separated, joined different ships and were never reunited!)[8] After watching the men go through their drill Moore made 'the most intimate inspection of every man'. Afterwards, calling the officers together, the Commander-in-Chief told them he had 'never seen a body of men in finer order than your regiment: they appear more like a picture of a battalion than actual men bearing arms'.[9] The 28th, however, were not cardboard cut-out soldiers, witness General Paget's famous remark some weeks later on the retreat to Corunna on seeing the men's disappointment at the enemy's reluctance to attack them: '28th, if you don't get fighting enough, it is not my fault'![10]

In a General Order of 15 October Moore, who was anxious to ensure the good discipline of his army as it entered Spain, instructed his troops to keep by their respectful behaviour the goodwill of the Spanish population. As a compliment to the host nation the army would wear the red cockade in their head-dress in addition to their own badges. Worried about the question of camp followers and the related supply position, Moore also ordered his commanding officers to try and prevent as far as possible women from accompanying their menfolk on the impending long march inland, during which, on account, for instance, of the shortage of carts, they would be exposed to excessive hardship and distress. The numbers of women usually allowed abroad – four or six to a company – had been greatly exceeded on this expedition when women had slipped surreptitiously on to the fleet transports at home or had reached Portugal in some other way. Further, Moore had even offered to send women back home, but few accepted his offer, and the majority, even those pregnant, refused to leave their men, despite knowing that they would only be entitled to half-rations (and their children to quarter).[11]

Moore decided that, as he had been ordered to drive the French, whose main body of troops was believed to be behind the Ebro, out of Spain, his first objective should be Valladolid. There he planned to combine with the reinforcements sent him of 10,000 men under Sir David Baird. This veteran soldier – he had endured four years' captivity in an Indian dungeon during the Mysore wars – had just landed at Corunna, where the Spanish authorities had, for no good reason, delayed the men's disembarkation, to Baird's great annoyance. In making his decision Moore must have realized that he was plunging into the heart of Iberia without any real knowledge of the state of the Spanish army, with whom he was required to cooperate, or of the numbers of French troops he would be facing. In fact the enemy strength in Spain would soon reach 300,000 men. But the British army as a whole had great faith in Moore and his professionalism. What endeared him to his officers, as a young ensign in the 28th reported, was his

constant habit of speaking to every officer of his army whom he met, whatever his rank, asking such questions as tended to elicit useful information, and in the most good-humoured and courteous manner.[12]

Nevertheless there was a small minority of officers who were not so sure of Moore's ability to be decisive and firm.[13]

Certainly it was no easy task that the army had been given, although this would scarcely have been appreciated by the rank and file as the leading regiments cheerfully left Queluz on 11 October for the Spanish frontier. Their march towards Spain was, of course, without opposition, for there were by then no French troops left in Portugal. Moore's men merely had to contend with the autumnal weather, the poor roads and finding enough to eat. Unlike the French, who lived off the country, the British had to pay the local people for their provisions.

Bevan told Mary, when he wrote to her on 13 November from Ciudad Rodrigo, just over the border into Spain, that their march from Lisbon via Abrantes and Guarda, had been a 'long and fatiguing' 200 miles. They were about to move on another 68 miles, according to Bevan, to Salamanca before reaching Valladolid. Nevertheless he was in quite buoyant mood.

This cold weather agrees wonderfully well with me. We have fared well on the road . . . the difference in the manners of the people [in Spain] is wide from those of Portugal. Especially in cleanliness which to an Englishman is an important consideration – but they do not give us anything to eat which the others [Portuguese] did.[14]

Sometimes there were moments almost of homesickness in his letters home. After all he had been away, he reminded his wife, 'for nearly nine months' (actually it was seven, though it must have seemed longer). Thus he laments that

our long separation I well know will give you many uneasy hours so does it to me – but I hope we shall after this be more together. A soldier's life is indeed not very stationary as you have already experienced. But I think we have been more unlucky than is usually the case. I hope for better times.[15]

At Ciudad Rodrigo the town turned out to welcome the army with shouts of 'Viva los Ingleses'.[16] This manifestation of joy at seeing the British troops arrive was rather against the trend elsewhere in Spain. Thus at the next major stop, Salamanca, Bevan could not be enthusiastic about the troops' reception by the people. In this ancient city, the army, now somewhat stalled for various reasons, spent upwards of a month. One effect of this was that Bevan was provided with more time to reflect. He was not opposed, as we have seen, to a good grumble:

> My billet is a most uncomfortable one – they give me nothing and I believe wish me at the Devil as often as they look at me – I am rather astonished that they do not at such a juncture as the present treat us with a little more hospitality – I shall be most happy when we advance as I always think that as we proceed we are getting nearer home, which I shall rejoice to do after a glorious campaign.[17]

Other officers had similar experiences over their quarters, for instance when in private houses they found themselves excluded from the life of the family and were left to eat their meals on their own. As for the other ranks, who were quartered in the convents, it was the same. They tried to make friends with the populace but without success. This response to visiting soldiery was perhaps not so surprising from a proud and haughty race. Nevertheless, the impression was firmly gained by the British, at least as seen through Bevan's eyes, that their army was not wanted by their allies in Spain. In fact, it is true to say that what the Spanish really wanted from the British were funds and equipment, not men.

Bevan had a chance in Salamanca of seeing some of the sights and in his description of them to Mary he showed some enthusiasm for architecture and art:

> The country since we have entered Spain has been very fine and I think improves as we advance as do the roads – Salamanca is but a poor city, principally conspicuous and indeed famous for its Colleges and Universities. Here is also a very fine Cathedral esteemed the most so of any in Spain the style of the Building is Gothick and certainly most beautiful – Amongst other things it contains a very fine painting by Titian (descent from the Cross) and two others said to be very excellent by an inferior painter (Spagnoletti). After the Cathedral is the Irish College, a stupendous building originally raised by the Jesuits for their own residence but upon the expulsion of that order from Spain the college was presented by the King to the Irish of which nation there are now several students; and I imagine that in the time of profound peace this is one of the seminaries for the Catholick Clergy of Ireland – there are no places of public amusement – a company of Comedians are permitted to be here during the times of vacation in the colleges, but at present the studies are going on or we should have seen the best performers from Madrid.[18]

Curiously Bevan does not mention in his description the magnificent square of the Plaza Mayor, which ought to have caught his eye.

Besides these views on Salamanca, he gave Mary some of his thoughts on the military situation. Thus, Moore was at Salamanca with about 12,000 men, awaiting the arrival of the artillery which had been delayed by bad roads. Then he mentioned a rumour that Napoleon was in Spain near Burgos with 120,000 men. This was, however, possibly a 'trumped up story', he felt. Then the French had lately gained some advantages over a Spanish force commanded by Joachim Blake (their general of Irish extraction), but Bevan heard that these were not of any great importance and warned that the opposition paper *Chronicle* would re-echo the exaggerated statements in the *Moniteur*. When Baird joined Moore Bevan ventured that

> the English force will consist of, I believe, 40,000 men. Do you not think it will take some few Frenchmen to beat such an army and Sir John Moore?[19]

These observations are interesting not so much for their precise accuracy – he was usually near the mark, however – as for his lively comments on what was going on and for his loyal belief in Moore.

Moore in fact was facing some difficult military-cum-political decisions. While he waited at Salamanca for Lieutenant-General John Hope and his guns and cavalry to come up from Portugal by a longer and supposedly better road than the one he had used, and for Baird to reach Astorga, 100 miles to the north, Moore began to be uneasy about his predicament. He was still without half the force he commanded and he lacked, as usual, any decent intelligence about the enemy. So far he had received little if any encouragement from his Spanish ally. On the contrary Spanish opposition to the French seemed to have been disintegrating after defeats suffered in November by Blake at Espinosa and Castaños at Tudela. Moreover Moore was not in regular communication with any Spanish general and, unbelievably, no overall Spanish Commander-in-Chief had been appointed. Indeed at this time Spain has been described as a country without armies, generals or government. But now the Emperor himself was about to make his presence felt in Spain, although Moore was not yet aware of just what was in store for him and his troops. Napoleon reached Bayonne on 3 November and Vitoria on 14 November, before travelling swiftly on towards Madrid.

At this juncture, to the consternation of most of his generals, but not to Baird or to Hope, who had now just arrived at Salamanca, Moore decided, perhaps uncharacteristically, to retreat to Portugal with his main army and to send Baird back to Corunna. This was a bad moment for the British force anxious above all to fight the French.

But then Moore had second thoughts. There were several reasons for this. First he was encouraged by a report which was to prove misleading that Madrid was preparing to offer stout resistance to the advancing Napoleon. Then he learnt that the Marqués de la Romana was at the head of a large Spanish force at Leon. So, mindful of his role that he was to do all he could to help Spain, he changed his mind. Then, in spite of hearing of the fall of Madrid to Napoleon on 4 December, Moore decided to move northwards towards Valladolid, as originally intended, and thereby get astride Napoleon's lines of communication. This he hoped would draw the French away from the Spanish capital and from the south of the country. Also he cancelled his previous order to Baird. It was a bold and even risky move that Moore embarked on, particularly considering the huge number of French troops now in Spain.

With much relief on 11 December the army began to advance to the north-east. Bevan too would have been pleased that something positive was now happening. Three days later at Alaejos Moore learnt that Marshal Soult with a force of less than 18,000[20] was on the Carrion River about 85 miles north in a somewhat exposed position. This force seemed to offer the British a worthwhile target. Might not Moore, having joined forces with Baird, be able to attack Soult before Napoleon could successfully intervene? Evidently Moore thought so, relishing the idea of smashing Soult. He, therefore, for a second time, changed his plans, this time by slightly modifying the direction of his advance. On 21 December he reached Sahagun, at about the same time as Baird arrived there, and made his headquarters in a wing of the Benedictine convent. In clearing Sahagun of enemy elements just before Moore's arrival, Lord Paget, Edward's elder brother and an outstanding cavalry leader, who would famously lose a leg at Waterloo, had a successful encounter with 600 French dragoons. In a decisive though small-scale victory the 15th Hussars inflicted severe casualties on the French and took 170 prisoners, including two colonels and eleven other officers.[21]

The combined British force at Sahagun now numbered some 29,000 men reorganized by Moore into four infantry divisions under Baird, Hope and Fraser, with the Reserve under Edward Paget. In addition there were two light brigades under Craufurd and Alten, while the cavalry division was commanded by Lord Paget. The 28th had been put in the Reserve as Bevan had hoped and as he told Mary when writing his last surviving letter to her from Spain. Indeed the Reserve were destined to play a staunch and valiant role during the army's retreat to Corunna.

Napoleon, confused momentarily over Moore's movements (thinking in fact he was heading back to Portugal), now suddenly heard that the British general was threatening his rear. On 19 December the Emperor, about to leave for the Portuguese frontier and no doubt aiming eventually to take Lisbon, changed his mind and decided to move against Moore instead. Within a few days he and his Guard were at the foot of the pass over the Guadarrama Mountains north-west of Madrid leading to Salamanca. In driving snow this awesome soldier was personally leading his men up to the summit of the pass before descending to Villacastin, 100 miles or so from Sahagun. The gap between the armies was closing and Napoleon was now poised to strike at the British with, including Soult's force, 80,000 men,[22] and so avenge the defeats inflicted on French armies at Alexandria, Maida in Italy and Vimeiro.

A game of cat and mouse had in fact begun between Moore and Napoleon. Moore, on learning that a large French force commanded by the Emperor himself was coming up fast behind him, that his supply route back to Portugal had consequently been cut off and that there would be no help forthcoming from the ineffectual Spanish armies, reluctantly decided that there was only one way he could extricate his own army from the Emperor's grasp. He and his troops would have to retreat the 250 odd miles back to Corunna and Vigo, despite the onset of severe winter weather and the many difficulties, logistical and other, which would arise on the way. The troops, when they heard of this decision, were in a state of sullen disbelief, almost of mutiny, at the turn of events, unable to understand the necessity for retreating.

There was no time to be lost. Hope and Fraser left Sahagun on Christmas Eve for Benavente and Astorga taking at first a south-westerly road in the direction of the French, who had been resting at Tordesillas just 60 miles to the south. Moore with the light brigades and the Reserve, and therefore the 28th and Bevan, set off on Christmas Day, following Hope's column. His first objective – and this explained the direction of his march – was the all-important bridge over the River Esla at Castrogonzalo, some 45 miles from Tordesillas, which his troops, excepting Baird's who were taking a more northerly line to Astorga, would have to cross. Fortunately Moore was too quick for Napoleon, but only just. By the time the Emperor's cavalry had reached Castrogonzalo Moore had managed to get his army across the river and, after Captain John Fox Burgoyne, a future field-marshal, had blown up the bridge watched by a party of chasseurs, was on his way to Astorga. It was a close-run thing. But the retreat had only just begun.

CHAPTER SIX

From Sahagun to Corunna

As far as we know Charles Bevan left no written record of his experiences during the retreat to Corunna. He never kept a diary on campaign and, obviously enough, there was no time for writing letters home during the retreat.

So there is no direct evidence from him of the part he played during that horrendous march of 250 miles over difficult mountain roads in the depth of winter. But his regiment was, as we have said, in Paget's Reserve and this division, as the army's rearguard, played a crucial role in keeping at bay the ever-threatening enemy cavalry and skirmishers which followed in the wake of Moore's disordered and increasingly ill-disciplined force. The 28th Foot was involved in the principal actions with the French all the way to Corunna.[1]

Some 90 or so years after the Battle of Corunna Georgina Bevan, a great-granddaughter of Charles Bevan, wrote a novel about her forebear, giving it the rather unpromising title *It May Have Happened Thus*. She was a woman with a literary bent and wrote short stories, some of which were published. However, her novel, although she tried to interest publishers in it, never saw the light of day. The book proves to be a good read, if at times a trifle sentimental for today's tastes. Clearly, as the text reveals, Georgina had access to some of Bevan's letters to Mary. In addition we may presume that Georgina had heard from her family, especially from her father, Captain George Dacres Bevan of the Royal Navy, tales of her great-grandfather's deeds in the Napoleonic wars.

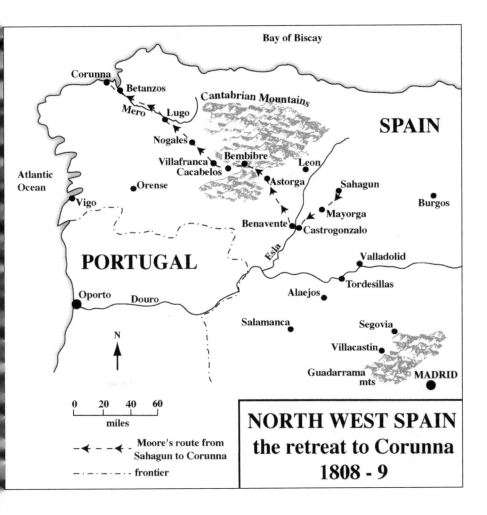

NORTH WEST SPAIN
the retreat to Corunna
1808 - 9

0 20 40 60
miles

Moore's route from
Sahagun to Corunna

frontier

With some skill and intuition Georgina reveals in her novel, or so it seems to this writer, quite a convincing understanding of Bevan and his character. This she has demonstrated in dealing with the known facts of Bevan's life and in the fiction she has woven round them. Consequently her story hangs together and is mostly credible. In addition, her knowledge of the general history of the Napoleonic wars and of Moore's campaign in Spain is sound. Georgina's account of the retreat to Corunna certainly adds to the authenticity of Bevan's story, particularly in the absence of any material about his part in the episode, so here follow some appropriate excerpts from her book.

While Bevan was away in Portugal and Spain in 1808, his wife Mary lived with her parents, Admiral and Mrs Dacres, at their house, Money Hill, in Rickmansworth. The following scene from the novel is thus set by Georgina in the Dacres' family house at about the beginning of February 1809, a short time after the army had returned from Corunna. Mary, so the narrative of the novel runs, had received a letter from Charles from Portsmouth to say he had arrived back in England and would soon be with her. She has now returned from an afternoon visit to the local village shop with her sister Eleanor.

The first thing that caught Mary's eye [in the hall] *was an officer's cloak and hat lying across a chair.*

"Charles must have come!" she cried to Eleanor and hardly were the words out of her mouth than the dining room door opened and there he stood on the threshold. But oh! how changed! The waning afternoon light accentuated the shadows under his eyes and made him look pale, gaunt and drawn, his uniform was shabby and dirty — no more signs of the spruce officer.

"Oh! Poor Charles!" and full of love and pity, she ran to him burying her face in his shoulder . . .

"My dear, my dear, what have they done to you?" Mary asked, looking searchingly into his face.

Charles bent down, kissed her and drew her into the dining room.

"*Come, my love, don't worry about my appearance. Tell me how you are and our dear little men. I have not heard anything about you, since I left Salamanca*".

"*Oh, nothing has happened to us, my dear, we are all well and our little family as perfect as may be . . . But you look as though you had gone through something terrible. Tell me, was there any fearful disaster?*"

"*Ah, Mary, it is a long story and not a pleasant one. It makes one wonder how any man of keenness and feeling can be induced to take command. The Government gives you no help, only expects you to carry out its ill conceived plans and blames you if there is disaster. Nay, it ignores your advice and misleads you. Your subordinate officers criticize your every action and fail at the critical moment and still you are blamed – Oh! 'tis as well Moore died when he did!*"

Charles spoke with extreme bitterness; in the strength of this bitterness, he had almost forgotten Mary. She had never seen him look like this and it troubled her,

"*But you are home now with me, my darling. Do not let past troubles spoil our present relief in being together.*"

Charles turned to her, his look softened and he caught both her hands in his.

"*My dearest and best of friends, I am a selfish brute. Do not let us talk about it any more just now. Later you shall hear the whole history. Let me see my dear little fellows and they and my good fellow here,*" *pressing Mary's hand,* "*will chase away all melancholy.*"

Little Charles, now a sturdy little chap of three, did not recognise his father, whom he had not seen for nearly a year and stood shyly by his Mother's knee with his finger in his mouth. Tom, just able to toddle about, was not so overawed and ran up to Charles, consenting to be taken on his knee and to play with his tunic buttons. Edward lay on his Mother's lap, gurgling and kicking, sublimely indifferent to the doings of the others.

"*What a large family!*" *exlaimed Charles, laughing,* "*I feel a regular pater familias. Come on, my son, you mustn't be frightened of me. Don't you remember the games of horses we used to have? Come and have a ride on my knee. See, I'll give Tom one first!*" *Tom enjoyed this so much that it fired Charlie to do the same, so he overcame his shyness and was soon romping with his father in fine style. But Mary could tell by Charles' face that his nerves were in no condition to stand children for long, so after a while, she rang for Elizabeth* [the nursery maid] *to take them back to the nursery.*

"And you have been quite happy here with your people?" he asked.

"Yes, as happy, if you can call it that, as I could be without you. Everyone has been kindness itself. Dear Cousin Shaw has sent such nice presents for the children. I visited her several times when I was in London."

"And my Mother and sisters—?"

Mary looked rather uncomfortable.

"I called on Mrs Bevan two or three times, but she was always out or lying down and whenever I begged her to come and see the children, she always had some excuse – but the girls I saw often – at least Caroline – Julia is still so hard and reserved – I cannot make her out at all" . . . .

By the time Admiral and Mrs Dacres returned, Charles presented a better appearance. Mary produced some clothes of his, that she had been keeping against his return, the shabby old uniform was relegated to the bottom of a trunk and, washed, shaved and clean, he was more recognisable. . . .

Later on in the evening, after a good dinner, Charles, feeling that he must pour out his story, broke down his reserve and when the whole party was gathered round the drawing room fire, he recounted his experiences. . . .

"Twas the false information about the Spanish forces that was our undoing. The Government was hoodwinked as to the amount of help available – hoodwinked as to the size and efficiency of that army. We met some of Romana's division up at Benavente and such ragamuffins you'd scarcely believe any one would call them soldiers – a regular Falstaff's army – many without accoutrements or even shoes – their muskets exploding and all looking worn out, and the other divisions were reported to be no better. . . .

"No, the whole expedition was sent out from England on wrong premises and so Sir John found, when he got over the frontier. At Salamanca the news filtered down all the ranks, that defeats had taken place and that

the French Army would be marching on us in force, undeterred by the Spanish. Moore knew, of course, that Baird's division had been so delayed – again by Spanish muddles and jealousy, that it might not join up with us in time. But, of course, we did not know that". . . . .

Georgina, after describing the march from Salamanca to Sahagun, continues her narrative about how the army, leaving Sahagun on Christmas Day, at length reaches Benavente.

"Well, off we started back to Benavente through pouring rain, sticking knee deep in mud, curses and discontent on every side – the ox waggons got fixed in the mud and it was awful to see the poor beasts trying to extricate themselves and being goaded and thrashed and sworn at. We of the 28th and the other regiments in the Reserve were pretty steady – a strict watch was kept over the men and the officers were not allowed to indulge in that tittle tattle about their superiors, that eternal disagreement with every order, that is ruin to discipline. Good God! Sir, if you had heard some of these trumpery little rascals of officers, criticising a splendid Commander like Moore, it'ud have made your blood boil. . . . .

"The result of that was that the men got out of hand and broke loose, whenever they had a chance. Granted they were badly fed, that the marches were of the hardest . . . . *Still the officers ought to have controlled themselves and the rank and file. Instead of which they stood by helpless, whilst they saw the men plundering right and left and clubbing the natives, if they objected – [and] stripping stores of food and drink – Why at Benavente I think it was, men were discovered tearing the woodwork from the houses to make themselves fires! Moore discovered this when he came up and gave the officers a sound rating, and issued a general order on the subject – but it did not do much good, the poison had worked too effectively."*

"They wanted stringing up, the whole lot of them," remarked the Admiral.

"There would have been very few left if you started on that game, sir. However, we were not allowed to get to Benavente without a brush with the French – their cavalry had been pursuing us all the time, yapping at our heels, but luckily they were not certain of our lines of retreat. But at the bridge across the Esla at Castro Gonzalo – close to Benavente – they came

61

on us. Most of our regiments had got over and were marching across the plain to Benavente – the bridge had been ordered to be blown up, but, as you might expect from what I told you, these orders had not been carried out promptly and there were a frightful lot of stragglers to be got over. Paget's cavalry kept the Frenchies at bay, while Crauford's men worked at destroying the bridge and it was a devil of a strong one. It was night before it was really accomplished. Torrents of rain were coming down and the river was in flood, the remainder of the men and our Reserve had to get over single file on planks thrown across. By God! It was a touch and go, but it was so dark, that, although it was terribly difficult for us, the enemy could not perceive our movements and at midnight we were all over, and the French cursing, on the other side. . . .

Next day we started for Astorga across a miserable desolate country, rocky and bare, but not much in the way of mountain. We expected to find stores and equipment there, something to fill our bellies with and to cover our feet. With this prospect discipline had got better and the men marched in fair order. But, would you believe it, when we reached the place, we found that the Spanish division from the north [under Romana] had taken refuge there and the town was filled with these miserable rapscallions. There was such confusion and crowding that no proper distribution of stores was possible! Our men had also an idea that Moore was going to make a stand there and many of the officers had the impudence to spread round that it was his duty to do so – but he knew his own mind and had his own reason for refusing. You see, he had not enough bread to carry him two days' journey, let alone other equipment and, also, the Spanish troops were riddled through with typhus and no good, in fact a danger to our men. So on the 30th we took to the road again and the devil a bit of discipline was there left in many of the regiments. We, the Rearguard, marched on the 31st and only just in time, as on New Year's Day Boney entered the town. This was the worst bit of the march. Snow was falling thick and we were heading straight for the mountains and such mountains, a great range rising sheer, peak after peak, that is the welcome Galicia gives one. The snow lay thick up there – it was pouring with rain, rain that stung you with cold and nearly froze on you; under foot, the roads had been churned to slush, mud and filth by the troops that had *preceded us. There were plenty of signs of these troops, I can tell you. Drunken stragglers, stragglers dropping with cold and fatigue – for, mind you, many of the men were without shoes and in rags – horses that had had to be shot, waggons hopelessly stuck, perhaps with unfortunate women and children, soldiers' families who were following the Army, inside them and the poor wretches even sitting hopelessly by the side of the road – a trail of misery – We marched into Bembibre, hoping for once to get a night under shelter. But, good God! I have never seen such sights! There are enormous wine vaults at this place – it is a centre of the wine trade – and the troops got wind of the fact. They broke free from all control and absolutely filled themselves with liquor! We had to march over their drunken bodies, every street was blocked with these beasts, either lying like logs or staggering about, yelling out bawdy songs, groaning, vomiting – ugh! It makes me retch to think of it – the women, too, joining in this filthy orgy. And not only soldiers but officers as well! Every house was occupied and the wine vaults were strewn with bodies. There was no room for us and we had to bivouack outside the town in snow and rain. That did not make us feel in a better temper with the dirty swine. The next day it was our pleasant duty to wake up these precious troops and clear them out, and we didn't mince matters, many of them got the flat of my sword and pretty hard too – and the enemy was pressing on full tilt only about twelve hours behind. However, we got them cleared out somehow, though many were left behind and taken prisoner or cut down by the French cavalry and it served them right. I heard that there were horrible scenes outside the town, when these poor wretches lost their heads, threw away their muskets and rushed hither and thither to escape the slashing of the French swords."*

Admiral Dacres looked horrified.

"How is it that Moore could not cope with insubordination better than that – Lord, I would have strung 'em all up on the yard's arm. In the Navy we'd clap 'em under irons."

"Yes, sir, and it would have done the whole Army good, but when you're flying from the enemy at the rate we were, there really isn't time. At Villafranca, Moore happened to ride in when disgraceful scenes were going on again. He caught a man red-handed and had him hanged at once and

no nonsense about it. And in the Reserve, General Paget was giving us a warning about not keeping a firm hand on the men whilst we were at Cacabelos, when three men were brought in – thank goodness, they did not belong to the 28th – who had been caught marauding. Paget ordered them to be hung then and there and we were all lined up to witness it, but at that moment, thank God, for I was dreading the beastly sight – a galloper came up to say the French were close on us and sure enough we heard shots – so the men were released on promise of good behaviour. No, when the officers are insubordinate, it is difficult dealing with the men. We had a little skirmish here, for some French infantry as well as the cavalry, appeared and obliged us to hold the town. . . . At night Moore drew us off to Villafranca – the action had just retarded the French advance and given the main Army a few more precious hours. The road after Villafranca was appalling and the sights the worst we had yet encountered in the way of misery – but perhaps I shall not harrow you with further description?"

"Yes, yes, go on, Charles, we can stand it."

"All right then, but of course no mere relation of the events can bring back the real horror as I saw it and you can be thankful for that. Many cavalry horses had broken down – poor brutes, their shoes had worn out and been cast and our splendid Commissariat never thought of supplying either nails or hammers to put on new ones with. The consequence was that these horses went lame and had to be shot and their bodies lay all over our road to rot and be trampled in. But the poor soldiers' wives with their wretched children clinging round them, dying of cold and starvation – we did as much for them as we could but that wasn't much, for we were short of clothes and very short of food. One poor woman was being brought to bed on the road. Lord! I can hear her groans now – we tried to help her but there was no time to spare, we had to press on and on and on. The strange thing was that we heard afterwards that the woman had regained the Army with her baby in some miraculous manner – she turned out to be a sergeant's wife. We had a bit of luck, in that we met a Spanish convoy of clothing, which we promptly appropriated or it would have fallen straight into French hands. It did not take long to fit ourselves out and very badly we needed it, I can tell you! The French were at our heels all that day,

but never overtook us. But at Nogales their cavalry were sleeping within a mile of us; poor brutes, they were as much done up by the march and privations as we were!

"We had two little skirmishes on the way to Lugo — the rearguard had to keep going pretty quick, I assure you, not to have their heels bitten and just as we were pressing on as quick as we could, we came upon the waggons, containing the treasure chest £25,000. They had stuck hopelessly in the mud and to prevent the money falling into the enemy's hands, the barrels containing the cash had to be rolled down a precipice. Think of that, £25,000 lying at the bottom, no good to anyone and our men all short of pay! I believe some of the Frenchies managed to fill their pockets. However, they had more time. The fool of an officer in charge of the treasure had not provided himself with fresh animals and this was the result! Ah well! Worse things happened than that!"

"Rather an expensive mistake, I fear. How in the world did the men get paid without any specie?"

"They didn't get paid, that's all. All the food had to be paid cash down, so all the coin had to be kept for that. The country between Nogales and Lugo was not so mountainous — masses of vineyards and stone walls — herds of tall thin brown swine, rushing off whenever they caught sight of us. Nothing could be procured from the inhabitants, except occasionally, if one was lucky, a bit of salt fish or a basin of broth, caldo gallego they call it — funny tasting stuff. We marched on to Lugo and halted a few miles out. Moore was there already and although he had considered it as an alternative, he decided not to engage the enemy there but to press on to Corunna. We of the Reserve were not allowed any rest, as the enemy was too near and Sir John wished to give them the slip and clear out at night, so, leaving the watch fires burning, the troops were all marched off. The weather was terrible — rain, wind, everything to daunt us. Lots of the troops lost their way and wandered about the lanes round Lugo till the morning, drenched to the skin. The Reserve was the only division that struck the main road right. . . .

"Well, this losing of the way made the discipline worse than ever and it was more of a rabble than an army that entered Betanzos on January 9th. Hundreds of men were left on the road to die or be taken prisoner. The

Reserve had to halt outside Betanzos and remain in position all night to cover the main troops. A halt was called for a day to give us a rest – we were all suffering badly – I assure you I was so cold when I dismounted that I could hardly stand up and the poor old Colonel was absolutely stiff with rheumatism and as for the men's feet, they were in a shocking condition, half frozen and lacerated. On the 11th we marched out of Betanzos somewhat refreshed and, thank goodness, the weather changed. We had got near the sea and instead of snow and frost we found mild weather, oranges and lemons, a real beautiful spring feeling. It heartened us all up. We met the French under Soult, while we were protecting the engineers, who were blowing up the bridge over the Mero, but we had to retire. However, we all managed to clear before the Marshal had time to collect his troops and on January 11th the main body marched into Corunna. We stayed at El Burgo after having destroyed the bridge. . . . Moore must have felt sickened, when he watched the main body of troops march into Corunna, a dreadful looking army, miserable, spiritless, ragged. All the commanding officers had a word from the General and sometimes it could not have been a complimentary one.

"Luckily for us there were a quantity of stores in Corunna that had never been distributed and Moore was able to re-arm the troops with good serviceable muskets. This was a mercy, as a battle was evidently imminent. On the 13th we had been withdrawn from El Burgo and marched to our position near the village of Oza on the road to Corunna, protecting the right flank of our Army and the French were in the meantime at work repairing the bridge at El Burgo, preparatory to advancing on us.

"You see, the transports had not all arrived at Corunna and the few that were there were being filled with the sick to get them off as soon as may be. But, owing to the delayed arrival of the main body of ships, there was practically no possibility of the rest of the troops embarking, before the enemy should be on us. On the 14th a few more transports arrived [in fact 100 transports arrived that evening], guns, horses and cavalry were shipped into them. This intelligence must have excited the French to action. They were not going to let us slip from their grasp, and on the 15th they attacked our outposts."

In her narrative Georgina now turns to the actual Battle of Corunna, which took place on 16 January. She does not, however, say what precisely was the role of the Reserve Division, or therefore of the 28th in the fighting. Nor does she allow Bevan to say anything about his part in the contest for Georgina saw her hero as an essentially modest man.

The 28th and 91st (Argyll and Sutherland Highlanders) were in Disney's brigade and were still placed in the Reserve. The men of that Division were told on the morning of 16 January that, as a reward for their distinguished conduct covering the retreat, they would embark first on the transports and make themselves comfortable.[2] So at 12 o'clock, after dining well, the men filed down through the town to the harbour. But it was not to be. At about 2 o'clock the movements of the French gave notice of an impending battle. At once the Reserve retraced their steps and were posted behind the centre of the line and then thrown into the thick of the developing battle in order to stop the advancing French from turning the British right.

Ground was gradually gained in the afternoon and Paget's men, now carrying all before them, forced the enemy to retire. On the left the desperate attacks of the French had been held, but only just; by dusk an important village was even retaken. It was at this moment that the 28th and 91st were sent forward to hold an isolated hill and keep the French cavalry at bay.[3]

On the right, where Bevan fought in the fiercest battle of his career, the 95th, 91st, 52nd (Oxfordshire and later the Greenjackets) and 28th were among those prominent in the army's heroic performance that day. The British losses had been 800–900 and the French more.[4] Moore himself had, late in the day, been terribly wounded while still in the thick of the battle and directing the fight. A round-shot had torn a deep hole in his left shoulder. He was carried to the rear but the surgeon could do nothing for him. Repeatedly he asked if the French were beaten. Before he died he had the satisfaction of being told by his devoted Military Secretary, Major John Colborne, that the enemy was indeed beaten.

Georgina finally ended her chapter on Corunna thus:

"There was no more fighting [after 16 January] . . . so [Sir John] Hope thought it wisest to withdraw us all and embark as soon as possible on board the transports, which by this time had arrived. We left a few picquets to keep the watch fires burning and retired into Corunna and started embarking, continuing all through the night. In the morning the French found the positions evacuated and advanced, firing a few shots. It was curious that those shots were fired just as Sir John Moore was being lowered into his grave – almost as though they had done it in honour of him. There isn't much more to tell, embarkation went on rapidly, although the French kept up a fire on the transports from the other side of the bay and caused dreadful confusion amongst some of the ships. By the 18th we had all cleared out leaving behind us the man for whom many of us would have laid down our lives."

There was a long pause.

"A sad story for the English to hear, Charles. I doubt not, however, it is better that Moore was killed than that he should be alive to hear all the talk and criticism, that will be going on now."

"Yes, sir, that is what makes us feel so bitter. If you had heard the vile stories that are being spread about him by these drunken rascals of soldiers who nearly undid us all, you should feel that he is better in his grave. And he himself was such a just man, he'd never punish, except when he knew it was necessary. Many commanders don't care if their subordinates get unjustly blamed, but he would always give a man a chance to clear himself. However, there it is – he's gone and God rest his soul."

Charles sat down exhausted staring miserably into the fire too much overcome to say more.

*   *   *   *

It was a rough passage home for the army. A heavy gale had blown in the Bay of Biscay and the convoy was scattered over hundreds

Charles Bevan. *(W. Colfer)*

2. Mary Bevan. *(W. Colfer)*

Mrs Richard Dacres and her daughter Lucy. *(W. Colfer)*

4. Mary *(seated)* and Eleanor. *(W. Colfer)*

5. An officer of the 4th
   Regiment of Foot, 1814.
   *(The King's Own Royal
   Regiment Museum)*

6. The Battle of Corunna, 1809.
   (from an aquatint by M. Dubourg: The King's Own Royal Regiment Museum)

'Soldiers of the 28th' by Thomas Hand, c.1803.   *(Soldiers of Gloucestershire Museum)*

8. The ruins of Fort Conception. *(W. Colfer)*

9. The bridge at Barba del Puerco today. *(W. Colfer)*

of miles of sea. The ships at length made landfall at the end of January, 1809, at a number of different ports along the south coast of England before unloading their cargoes of unkempt soldiery. The army's problems were compounded during its homecoming by the high incidence of typhus among the men. Some of the 28th landed at Plymouth and others at Portsmouth; then made their tired and unheroic way back to their quarters in Colchester.

CHAPTER SEVEN

The Scheldt

Within five months of returning from Corunna Bevan was off to serve on his sixth expeditionary force in the wars against Napoleon. This time his destination was Holland, more specifically the islands of the Scheldt estuary. The ultimate target lay further inland – the important port and dockyard of Antwerp. How had the government come to decide on this operation so soon after the terrible failure in Spain?

At the beginning of 1809 reports had reached Napoleon, while he was on the road to Astorga chasing after Moore in north-west Spain, that there was serious trouble brewing in Austria. At once he gave up his pursuit and hurried back to Paris, leaving it to Soult and Ney to finish off the British. The Austrians, he found, had been reorganizing their army and had raised aloft the flag of revolt against the French. With his customary speed and confidence, Napoleon moved against Archduke Charles of Austria, entering Vienna on 13 May, 1809. But he underestimated his enemy and consequently suffered a serious defeat on 22 May at the Battle of Aspern-Essling, when the renascent Austrians counter-attacked and inflicted no less than 20,000 casualties on his army, whose supplies of ammunition had been exhausted.

In the meantime the British government had not been inactive in once again planning to take offensive action against France. First they had been persuaded by Wellesley – he was still, as Chief Secretary for Ireland, a member of the government – in a memorandum he submitted to Lord Castlereagh, Secretary for War and

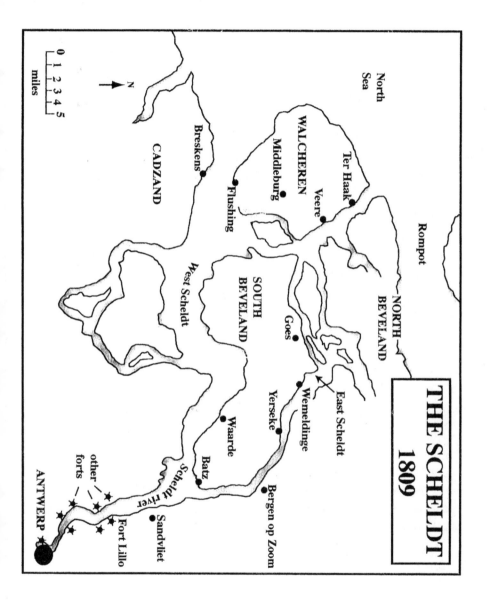

THE SCHELDT
1809

North
Sea

WALCHEREN

Middleburg

Ter Haak

Veere

Flushing

CADZAND

Breskens

Rompot

West Scheldt

SOUTH
BEVELAND

NORTH
BEVELAND

Goes

East Scheldt

Wemeldinge

Yerseke

Waarde

Batz

Bergen op Zoom

Scheldt river

other
forts

ANTWERP

Fort Lillo

Sandvliet

N

0 1 2 3 4 5
miles

71

the Colonies, that 20,000 British troops together with a reconstituted Portuguese army could defend Portugal whatever France managed to do in Spain. Wellesley's conclusions were accepted and he was made commander of a new expeditionary force, though his departure for Lisbon was somewhat blighted by a family disgrace. His brother Henry's wife, Lady Charlotte Wellesley, had just eloped with Lord Paget, the brilliant cavalry general whom we met in the previous chapter, causing a great scandal in London. Thus Wellesley could not take Paget with him to Portugal to command his Horse.

In Lisbon, which he reached in April, Wellesley found himself with some 23,000 men, including the garrison left in Portugal by Moore in the autumn of the previous year. Sensing an opportunity, Wellesley boldly moved north to Oporto to challenge Soult. Achieving surprise, he was able to cross the Douro, believed by the French commander to be impassable, and in doing so caught Soult and his men off guard. Thus was Portugal's second city freed and with a minimum of British casualties. For his part Soult beat a hasty retreat back into the Spanish province of Galicia. It was the moment for Wellesley to continue his advance, this time into Spain itself, a progress which was to result in his victory at Talavera, south-west of Madrid, in July.

While these events were unfolding in the Iberian peninsula, the government, inspired and driven by Lord Castlereagh, was sufficiently confident to plan a bold stroke across the North Sea. Something, it was felt, should be done to take the pressure off the Austrians. In deciding to aim at Antwerp the British would have the military objectives of capturing or destroying the enemy's ships either being built at Antwerp and Flushing or afloat on the Scheldt. In addition the arsenals and dockyards at Antwerp and elsewhere were to be destroyed, the island of Walcheren was to be reduced and if possible the Scheldt River was to be made unnavigable for enemy warships.

Despite warnings, especially one from the influential yet contentious Captain (later Rear-Admiral) Home Popham, about the need to launch an expedition before the weather deteriorated in the fickle approaches to the Scheldt, preparations for the enterprise went rather ponderously ahead. To the surprise of many, the second Earl of Chatham, the late William Pitt's elder brother, was appointed to command the 44,000-strong force being assembled. Chatham was essentially a politician not a soldier, though he had once commanded a brigade ten years earlier on the Helder expedition. He has been described as 'reflective rather than resolute and notorious . . . for his leisurely ways and epicurean habits'.[1] Really, it was a shocking appointment. Rear-Admiral Sir Richard Strachan, in command of the vast fleet of 400 transports and 200 warships required, had, in contrast to Chatham, the reputation of being an energetic, almost impulsive, officer. This particular combination of soldier and sailor did not bode well, nor in practice was it to be a success, as dissension over tactics came quickly to develop between the two commanders.

At the end of June the troops designated for the operation began to assemble at Dover. Taking six days for the 130 odd miles, the 28th, including a reinvigorated Charles Bevan, marched there from their barracks in Colchester in company with the two battalions of the 4th, with whom they were to be brigaded under Lord Dalhousie. Significantly, this was the first time there were no women with the army. The brigade was inspected by Sir John Hope, the divisional commander of the Reserve, who had stepped into Moore's shoes at Corunna, and then on 16 July the division embarked at Deal where the transports sailed to concentrate at the Downs off the Kent coast. This concentration of troops and ships had been, unhappily, a slow process and valuable time was thus lost.

Finally, on 28 July, a beautiful summer's day, the biggest expedition ever to leave English shores to that date sailed eastwards with a good wind for Holland, 65 miles away. Ramsgate cliffs were covered with people and it was reported, maybe a trifle optimistically, that officers on the ships could see through their glasses 'the waving of handkerchiefs by hundreds of fair hands'.[2]

While waiting on HMS *Lavinia* for, as it were, the starter's gun, Bevan cheerfully described to Mary life on board. First there was the captain of the frigate, Lord William Stuart, MP for Cardiff, who in Bevan's words was 'everything that was kind and hospitable' (it would no doubt have helped Bevan in his relations with Stuart that his father-in-law was a redoubtable admiral). He was also an officer with dash who would later distinguish himself in the Scheldt. The company, Bevan found, was congenial and the conversation stimulating. This is what he greatly relished. He might almost have been dining at an Inn of Court or at the High Table of an Oxbridge College. Among the passengers closeted with him were three agreeable and well-informed 'volunteers' who had come along to 'see the effects of the expedition'. One of them was a Mr Wood, a private secretary to Castlereagh. Somewhat in contrast, Colonel Belson, the C.O. of the 28th, a fine fighting soldier even if he was at times an over-harsh disciplinarian, was also of the party. These men, Bevan told Mary,

> constitute the regular dinner party – we go to bed at ten – yet get up at seven – the morning employed in walking the deck and reading – Sometimes in arguments in one of which I am always the Honourable opposition and always will be so: as far as my knowledge of the subject permits me to judge – There is only one man who could make me change my opinion of the matter and that would be from his superior knowledge of facts full as much as the Estimation in which I hold his judgment – that man is General Paget – The subject is Sir J Moore. Of course I have against me Lord Castlereagh's Secretary.[3]

This extract throws some light on Bevan's character, for instance his rebel streak and a determination to stand by his opinions. It confirms, too, his admiration for Edward Paget, his living hero. Moore was of course widely subjected to criticism for his handling of the Retreat, something which the government did little to allay. There were, however, those like Bevan who were strongly loyal to the man's memory and who believed he had saved the army from destruction, a verdict endorsed by most modern historians. In this same letter Bevan turns to matters literary:

We have just had a warm discussion, on what do you think? On the morality of Mr Monk Lewis's Monk. It was defended by one gentleman as a very excellent Moral work – You of course have never read it and therefore cannot judge of its morality: Thank God! This is the first and I hope it will be the last time I could hear so wonderful an opinion broached – I flatter myself I made some appropriate remarks and neat observations – How pleasant to argue on the side of virtue and morality and religion. You always compel me to argue a little on the other side; or we should have have no argument at all. I am sure this is paying you a very handsome compliment.[4]

This time Bevan was apparently on the side of the angels! The novel referred to was published in 1796 and had attained a considerable vogue. Its central character is a saintly superior of the Capuchins (a Roman Catholic order of friars) in Madrid who is ensnared by a wanton novice disguised as a boy. Now utterly depraved, he becomes enamoured of one of his penitents, finally killing the girl to escape detection. He is tortured by the Inquisition and enters into a compact with the devil to escape his death sentence.[5] Bevan may have been genuinely glad his wife had not read this lurid tale, but was evidently keen to tell her of the lively discussion about the book.

What Bevan did not comment on in his letter was Napoleon's crushing victory at Wagram over the Austrians. Since the battle had taken place on 5–6 July he might have been expected to have learnt of this major event, which resulted in Austria being knocked out of the war. The defeat of her ally must have been a blow to the

British who had conceived its expedition as an operation in support of the Austrians, but it was far too late to call the whole thing off.

The first military objective of the expedition seems to have been the seizure of both Flushing on the south side of the island of Walcheren and of the forts at Breskens on the opposite side of the Scheldt estuary. With these key points secured the way would be open for the escorted transports to continue up the western Scheldt and for a landing to be made at the eastern end of South Beveland or at Sandvliet on the mainland, or both, prior to marching on Antwerp. The precise methods of proceeding were left, in accordance with usual military practice in those days, in the hands of the Commander-in-Chief, Chatham.

Almost at once the expedition's plans went wrong. On the arrival of the fleet off the Dutch coast on 28 July a westerly gale sprang up, making a landing impossible on the south coast of Walcheren near Flushing. Consequently Popham, acting as pilot, was forced to take the fleet northwards into the quieter waters of the Rompot, north of the island of Walcheren, a manoeuvre he accomplished with skill. But now the ships and troops were on the wrong side of Walcheren. As a result the divisions commanded by Sir Eyre Coote had to disembark on 30 July on the north-eastern side of the island west of Fort Ter Haak, where some minor resistance was encountered from Irish and Prussian defenders. Flushing was some 12 miles march away via the towns of Veere and Middelburg. But there was virtually no opposition until the French halted the invading forces a few miles from the walls of Flushing. The town was at once invested and a siege began, culminating in a bombardment of the town by 50 guns on 13 August.

After the destruction of some 250 buildings and the infliction of heavy casualties, both civilian and military, the French commander surrendered the town and its garrison of 5,500 men two days later. The capture of Flushing had taken much longer than originally envisaged. However, the cost to the British was light:

50 killed and 208 wounded, as compared to 2,100 French casualties before the surrender.[6]

There had also been problems in the south side of the Scheldt where Lord Huntley's division had been due to land in Cadzand with the objective of capturing the forts at Breskens. But a variety of factors prevented a landing there, such as unfavourable winds and difficult currents. Then there seemed an insufficient number of craft to take the men ashore and there were problems over communications. Finally, the French had been able to reinforce their garrison. In the event Huntley's division lay idle in transports off shore for six days until 3 August and no landing was made. So the Breskens batteries were not neutralized. This had implications for the ability of the navy to sail freely up the West Scheldt. One historian believes that it was fortunate for the British that they did not land on Cadzand, as their position there might have become untenable.[7]

At least things went better for Hope's Reserve Division, which included the 28th, for, using the East Scheldt, they landed with no difficulty on 1 and 2 August near Wemeldinge on the north coast of South Beveland. They met no resistance as they marched energetically eastwards via Goes to Waarde and then on to Fort Batz, which, when it was entered on 2 August, they found to be deserted. The Dutch commander of troops on South Beveland had, just before, slipped away with some 900 men to Bergen op Zoom. The military position thus reached in South Beveland looked to be promising, with British forces now only 15 miles north of Antwerp, even if there was water as well as a string of forts between them and their ultimate objective.

Now there was anti-climax. From about mid-August onwards a kind of stalemate developed. Nothing was happening. British troops occupied the whole of Walcheren and South Beveland, but were making no progress at all towards Antwerp. Indeed at Fort Batz Disney's brigade had been twiddling their thumbs with virtually nothing to do for nearly a fortnight, except on one occasion, when they had to repel an attack by French gunboats. Obviously there had been a serious failure in the plan, as originally conceived, to move rapidly on to the mainland below Antwerp. Had an opportunity been missed? And if so, was this principally due to the failure to take Flushing earlier? King Louis of Holland reported from his headquarters at Bergen op Zoom to his brother the Emperor as late as 9 August that his position was very weak, and that, for instance, there was only one officer available to direct the defence of the important Fort Lillo.[8] *Per contra*, Bevan heard a report that King Louis had 16,000 men between Bergen op Zoom and Antwerp but no regular troops.[9]

The navy's role in the scheme of attack was critical. What had happened? Slightly mysteriously, Strachan, planning to sail his warships up the West Scheldt on 2 August, had delayed attempting the passage. Contrary winds may have been part of the explanation for the delay. Then on 11 August he sent Lord William Stuart upriver with ten frigates. In fine style they passed the batteries at Flushing and Breskens without suffering significant harm – just two men killed and nine wounded. Once Flushing had fallen Strachan believed immediate operations up the Scheldt would follow.[10] They did not.

The truth of the matter is that there was a failure between the army and navy properly to combine in carrying out the necessary operations. Chatham, with his slow pace of life, seemed to make little attempt to galvanize into action the forces under his command. At his first headquarters at Middleburg, during the early days of the Flushing siege, his tranquil regime reminded one irate colonel of the slow pace of life at headquarters in London. For instance a subordinate wishing to see Chatham, however urgent the matter might be, had to call between certain hours, send up his name and then await his turn.[11] No wonder after the campaign an epigram emerged neatly summing up the fearful state of affairs:

Lord Chatham, with his sword undrawn
stood waiting for Sir Richard Strachan

> Sir Richard, longing to be at 'em
> stood waiting for the Earl of Chatham.[12]

Certainly Chatham's indecisive ways could not have helped the already strained relations between the two commanders.

And what of Bevan in this campaign so far? According to one regimental history it was the 28th who had the very first encounter on land with the enemy, As the fleet lay off Walcheren on 29 July a telegraph was observed to be working on shore, no doubt relaying news of the appearance of so many ships. At once

> four companies of the 28th Regiment with carpenters of the squadrons were sent to silence it. The rigging and yards of the ships were covered with soldiers and sailors intently watching this little expedition. A picquet of the enemy was driven out and the telegraph mast and house were quickly levelled to the ground, the fall of the mast being received with three cheers from all the spectators.[13]

Even if Bevan was not in the landing party, he must have been, as a senior major, watching with intense and critical interest to see that the operation was properly carried out.

But the business of the 28th was in South Beveland. That consisted in moving rapidly eastwards in the direction of Antwerp. For Bevan there was no fighting or other dramatic events to describe in letters home to Mary. Nor did the unusual landscape of South Beveland, with its highly cultivated fields interesected with dykes and ditches, apparently afford him any immediate literary stimulation. After passing through Goes Bevan found himself at Yerseke, not so far from Bergen op Zoom, which lay six or seven miles away on the mainland across the sandbanks and the water. On 12 August Bevan told Mary, prosaically enough, that:

> we have been perfectly idle in the Fighting way but constantly moving and daily expecting to move to attack

Antwerp on the way to which there is a strong fort called Lillo to be taken. They have had too much time to prepare themselves. . . . Flushing is I fancy a tougher job than was expected and until that is taken our Fleet can not enter the Scheldt.[14]

He enclosed for Mary a plan of the islands (see p.81) over which he had taken some trouble even if it is not too easy to decipher all his annotations. He would not have gone into so much detail unless he was sure about the interest Mary took in his campaigning. Unhappily, and this must have been an oversight, he does not mark Flushing on his map!

The weather in August had been stormy and with sometimes oppressive heat. In the low-lying terrain stagnant water abounded. As the British troops lingered on in what were known to be the unhealthy islands of the estuary, they had to contend on Walcheren with the opening of the sluices by the French. Everywhere the waters rose, sending up a dense evil-smelling mist. It was a mosquitoes' paradise. Suddenly disease, deadly in its effect, struck the army. This was 'Walcheren fever', as it came to be called, a sickness by no means unknown in the Scheldt at the time of year. Writers have described the disease in different terms, but eclectically speaking it seems to have been a combination of malaria and dysentery with typhoid and typhus thrown in.[15] Bevan gave Mary a passing reference to the pestilence in his last surviving letter from South Beveland written on 25 August saying, 'The army is becoming very jittery, ague and xx fever in every Corps.' He was, we may assume, playing down the seriousness of the epidemic which had hit the army. Rifleman Harris, a veteran of the Napoleonic wars, described how strong young men 'seemed suddenly reduced in strength to infants unable to stand upright . . . they lay groaning in rows in barns'[16], while Captain Cadell of the 28th wrote:

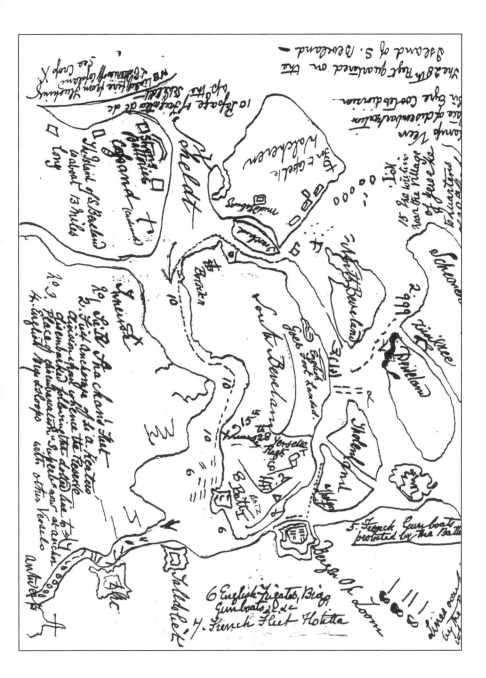

81

It was truly melancholy to behold the numbers that were cut off: every evening after dusk a string of eight to ten fine fellows were carried to their graves.[17]

After the campaign it was calculated that fever accounted for the deaths of 4,000 men compared to the 106 killed in action. Whatever Bevan really thought about the fever he was scathing about the leadership of the expedition, expecting there to be in due a course a 'rumpus', and stating 'business here has been horribly mismanaged. I have this moment heard that a Council of War has determined we return to England.'

Bevan was right about the expedition returning home. The decision to evacuate was taken at Batz, the army's final headquarters, on 28 August, by Chatham, his generals and the admirals. The number then on the sick list was more than 3,500 and rising daily (until in mid-September the figure was 8,200 men). Another reason for aborting the expedition was that the combined French-Dutch force on the left bank of the Scheldt was reckoned to have reached 35,500 men, too large a number for the much reduced British force to tackle with hopes of success.

Bevan did not have long to wait. The 28th, still in company with the 4th, sailed from Flushing, reaching Harwich on 16 September.

There was a curious regimental postscript to the campaign. Before it began three friends, C.O.s of the 4th, 20th (East Devonshires) and 28th regiments, Lieutenant-Colonels Wynch, Ross and Belson, had been arguing about the most suitable design for the regiments in respect of the recently authorized blue-grey trousers (instead of the previous white breeches). They agreed to do some experimenting during the Scheldt expedition, once they heard that their regiments were to be part of it. The 4th had tight trousers with black gaiters, the 20th wore them as overalls buttoned down the sides and the 28th had their trousers loose, with half-boots. On their return home in September the 4th's trousers were in rags while the 28th's, marching behind them into

Colchester, were nearly as good as when they started out. The successful pattern adopted by the 28th was, therefore, so it was claimed, copied by nearly every other regiment in the army.[18] Although there are some seventy-five surviving letters written by Charles Bevan to his wife, the great majority while he was on active service, never once does he mention dress or uniform. The subject was presumably of little or no interest to him!

Bevan was right about the 'rumpus' the failure of the Scheldt expedition would cause. First came the quarrel between Canning and Castlereagh. At the heart of this were the Foreign Secretary's long-standing efforts, some say intrigues, to have the War Minister removed from office. Now, at last, Canning saw a way: he could blame his rival for the Walcheren fiasco. Castlereagh, enraged by what he perceived to be the duplicity of Canning, challenged the Foreign Secretary to a duel. This was fought on Putney Heath on 21 September and resulted in Castlereagh wounding Canning in the thigh while Canning shot a button off the lapel of Castlereagh's coat![19]

The whole press of events was too much for the Prime Minister, the old Duke of Portland, who, after suffering a stroke, resigned his office. The government fell and Perceval became Prime Minister in early October just three weeks before Portland's death.

That did not quite end the 'rumpus', for in the year following the Scheldt expedition there was a parliamentary inquiry, which proved inconclusive, virtually a whitewash. No blame was attached to the military and naval commanders for the conduct of the operations and no censure was passed on ministers for deciding to send out the expedition in the first place.

It would have been revealing to know Bevan's views on this political-cum-military gallimaufry. He would have had some, and no doubt pungently expressed. But in the coming months his mind would become more firmly set than ever on his career. As he was about to leave for the Scheldt in July, he had written a fairly typical postscript in a letter to Mary:

Would to God we were off and back again that I was a Lt-Colonel and that we had a snug shop [house] near the sea.

Within a few months he was to achieve his ambition of becoming a lieutenant-colonel, but the house near the sea was denied him.

CHAPTER EIGHT

Ceuta

After the failure of the Scheldt expedition Bevan returned to Colchester to be reunited with his family. But it would be only a few months before he left England again for active service overseas.

For some time he had been bemoaning the fact that he was 30 years old, yet still not a lieutenant-colonel. Of course if you had both the influence and money you could purchase your promotion at a very young age. Edward Paget was a Lieutenant-Colonel at the ridiculously early age of 18. Ned Pakenham, whose sister Kitty married Sir Arthur Wellesley, was a major at 17! Both men were, of course, gilded youths, and had all the influence required. Bevan, not quite in the same social class as these two, did, however, have the money for his next promotion. It was the opening that he craved. Suddenly, or so it seemed, his luck changed. A vacancy occurred in the 4th Regiment, the King's Own, a regiment which, happily for Bevan, had two battalions. At the Scheldt the 1st battalion was commanded, as we have seen, by Lieutenant-Colonel Wynch and the second by Lieutenant-Colonel H.W. Espinasse. Following the retirement of Espinasse there was a vacancy in the second battalion and by the new year Charles Bevan had been appointed by purchase to the rank of lieutenant-colonel to command this battalion. Moreover, there was even an understanding that when Wynch became a brigadier, a promotion apparently in the offing and expected about the middle of the following year, Bevan would step up to command the 1st, and premier, battalion.

The 4th and 28th had been closely linked in the past five years, having been brigaded together on active service in a series of expeditions, namely those to Bremen, Gothenburg and the Scheldt. Both regiments had also for some years been stationed in Colchester when in England. They were therefore almost sister regiments. Bevan would have known all or most of the officers of the 4th, and so would have been well placed to hear about prospects in the Regiment. The fact that he was ambitious would not have been held against him, for his face fitted.

Bevan will have seen his promotion as a significant step forward in his career. While his pay increase was useful without being enormous – a lieutenant-colonel received 15s.11d a day compared to a major's 14s 1d[1] – his responsibilities were greatly increased. And the status of a lieutenant-colonel was undeniably higher than that of a major, denoting, especially in society, a distinct measure of success in the holder's career, even if that was not always deserved. Where Bevan found the money to fund the purchase of his promotion, or how much it cost, is not known. Maybe it came from his well-off cousin Mrs Shaw, or possibly his father had left money for that very purpose.

As to whether Bevan deserved his promotion on merit, the indications are that he was a competent soldier and that his command of a light company and then his post as a brigade major reflected his abilities both in the field and on the staff. Further, it is unlikely that this advancement would have come unless his performance during Moore's retreat to Corunna had been praiseworthy. It is possible that Charles' mentor Edward Paget had had, through his influence, a hand in his promotion. Paget was back in England at the time, having been seriously wounded in May at Oporto when he lost an arm and was invalided home. Paget's interest in Bevan and his career was, we believe, sustained after Corunna and the Scheldt.

The 4th Foot had a pedigree stretching back to the days of King

Charles II. It was originally raised, partly in London at Clerkenwell and partly in the West Country at Plymouth,[2] in 1680 for the defence of Tangier, a North African port which had passed from Portuguese into English hands as part of the dowry of Catherine of Braganza when she married Charles II. In the 18th century the regiment had fought in the War of the Spanish Succession, in the West Indies, in the Seven Years War and in the American War of Independence, as well as at home in both Jacobite risings and at Sedgemoor.

In January 1810 the second battalion of the 4th marched from Colchester to Portsmouth. They had been ordered abroad under their new commanding officer and embarked that month. While he waited for a decent easterly, Charles, pretending to be patient, kicked his heels around for about a fortnight, sometimes on board the 26-gun corvette *Jamaica*, sometimes on shore. He saw his old chief Paget, hobnobbed with Colonel Belson, Major Browne and Paymaster Dewes of the 28th who were at Portsmouth and who all made inquiries about Mary. Rather typically, he took pleasure in avoiding going to a ball and supper, but was pleased to dine with General Whetham, the Lieutenant-Governor of Portsmouth, for, to his evident satisfaction, the dinner cost him nothing! Just how he came to be sitting at the table of this luminary was not disclosed.

Quite apart from the pending separation from her husband, January was a bad month for Mary Bevan. After some years of failing health the old Admiral, to whom she was devoted, died, and her mother was for some time not well enough to leave London for the Dacres' house at Rickmansworth. Their younger son, James Dacres, was doing well in the navy, but at this time was without a ship, while Barrington, the older son, with whom Charles had been on friendly terms, had died a year or two before of fever probably caught while serving with the navy in the West Indies. On the brighter side Mary's sister Eleanor was now engaged to Jim Paterson of the 28th and they were soon to marry. About Mary's younger sisters, Jemima, Matilda and Lucy we hear little, though from time to time they get a kindly mention from Charles in his letters.

Before the convoy, of which the *Jamaica* was a part, cleared Yarmouth Roads and headed for Ushant, Bevan had the satisfaction of knowing from Mary that his mother-in-law was better. This was important to him because Mary, always the dutiful daughter, was anxious both about her mother and her siblings. Mary had also told Charles that she meant to take a house for six months in Rickmansworth during her husband's absence abroad. Charles had 'no objection' and wrote:

> I will send you money, that is when I have been long enough in the Regiment to have a balance . . . or I believe the best may well be to make them [the agents of the Paymaster] pay a certain sum into [your] hand, then you will have no trouble[3]

We must presume from these rather vague comments that, in the crowded circumstances of January, Charles simply did not have time to make proper arrangements for the financial support of his family and for their accommodation. There is a firm impression from Charles' letters over the years that, with his family commitments, he never had quite enough money. He was, on the other hand, thrifty, possibly with a slightly mean streak in him, and had to survive, as far as we are aware, on his pay. Money affairs would continue to worry him, especially as he wanted to educate his sons well and, inevitably, as was his wont, he passed his concerns onto Mary.

For the moment, and as the convoy sailed away down the Channel, Bevan was uncertain of the final destination of the Regiment. Was it to be Lisbon or Gibraltar? Actually it was to be neither, although the latter would be the first port of call. Even if Bevan was in comfortable quarters on the *Jamaica* under the command of Captain Lysaght – whom Charles liked, for, as was invariably the case, he got on well with naval officers – the voyage was an unhappy one. The convoy encountered a furious south-westerly gale not far from the Spanish coast. One transport was blown ashore and 300 men of the Regiment were taken prisoner by the French, including two captains, two lieutenants and the quartermaster.[4] The loss of the last named was to prove a serious blow to the new commanding officer when it came to settling his men into their new quarters on reaching their destination.

On arrival in Gibraltar it must have been a bit galling for Bevan to learn that the 2nd battalion of the 4th Foot was to be posted to Ceuta to garrison that small Spanish port on the North African shore. The requirement for this garrison had arisen as a result of Castlereagh's fears concerning the Straits of Gibraltar. If the French were to occupy Tangier and Ceuta they would be in a position to deny the British passage through the Straits. Ceuta, therefore, had to be kept safe from the French.[5] The role of the Regiment was clearly to be a static one, disagreeable to Bevan, though it might last, or so he must have hoped, for only a few months. In any case, soon enough he anticipated taking Wynch's place in the 1st Battalion, which was still at Colchester.

Bevan and his now very understrength battalion landed in Ceuta in March 1810. This Spanish enclave acted as a military post as well as a commercial port. In area it was small, though quite a bit bigger than Gibraltar which lay across the Straits some 17 miles away. Ceuta had been successively colonized by Carthaginians, Greeks and Romans. Once, in the days of the Byzantine Empire, it was independent, but, with its commercial importance, it fell under Portuguese rule in the 15th century before passing to Spain in 1580. The town, boasting a cathedral, lay at the foot of a huge citadel perched high up, and was a maze of narrow streets, passages and alleyways. The population was a mixture of Spanish, Berbers and other races and there was a Jewish community as well. Beyond the town lay a wild mountainous region inhabited by tribesmen with a fierce Berber warrior tradition. It was regarded as unsafe for travellers to venture far into that part of the country.

The reception accorded to the British troops was not, in Bevan's view, exactly friendly. The Governor and the local Junta were distrustful of them, doubting, for instance, that the British were keeping to their word about the number of troops landed, limited by an agreement with the Spanish authorities to 800 men, although Bevan told Mary that this number had not been exceeded. It may well have been rather irksome to the local people when the 4th Regiment marched into the citadel, as it had been agreed that they were entitled to do, and then hoisted the Union Jack, which, wrote Bevan, showing perhaps a touch of arrogance, 'We'll never cease to fly'. Later on, revealing a similar imperialist spirit, Bevan told his wife that he thought the British should retain a permanent hold on Ceuta.

Nevertheless Bevan decided the place was preferable to Gibraltar, where he had been stationed ten years or so before, especially climatically. He was also pleased that his men in the citadel had the best barracks he had ever come across and that they had 'plenty of grounds for exercise'. The officers did not fare as well, crammed three to a room, while Bevan himself had to be content with living in a summer-house, 'on suffrance' as he put it. At the end of March he was describing some of the problems he was encountering as commanding officer:

[The men] are all day long employed in getting our Baggage, provisions etc etc to the Citadel which is on the top of a very high and steep hill or a mountain. This work was too severe for our men and I have succeeded in getting the slaves or convicts who are sent here from various parts of Spain, chained together very much looking like Don Quixote's Friends for this purpose. You may suppose we are all in confusion. Not a cart or Mule in the place – No Fuel to cook the men's dinner – in short I am occupied from night to morning in Husbandry and from morning till night in this quest of a nature not very amusing – The [loss] of our Quartermaster falls very heavy on my shoulders. In a fortnight I hope we shall be settled. It is now half past six in the morning – I got up on purpose to write to you, for if I once go out of my appartment (which is a neat one) I am called upon by one horror or the other all day – having the honour to command all the troops in the Citadel which are, besides our own Regt, 50 Royal Veterans, sad fellows, and six Artilleryman . . .[6]

It is easy to feel some sympathy for Bevan, as he was being rushed off his feet during his first weeks in Ceuta. Quite apart from his quartermaster being a prisoner, he commented, 'My adjutant [is] sick in bed, my Paymaster at Gibraltar and [I have] a very young Regiment to command . . . but I am putting all my shoulders (sic) to the wheel'. The Adjutant, it seems, was often laid up with 'ague and fever'. At least in these early days in Africa there was plenty to do and Bevan was not bored. That came later.

Bevan did not usually find anything complimentary to say about the local population whom he described as often being 'lazy' or 'effeminate', nor about the Spanish refugees from the mainland who inhabited Ceuta in some numbers. These included grandees of the first rank, such as the Duke and Duchess of Medina Celi and the Duke of Osuna. Bevan's general antipathy to the Spaniards did not prevent him from attending a Governor's levée with his chief, Major-General Alexander Fraser, but this no doubt was a duty he had to perform. On the other hand he had to admit that some of the young ladies there were pretty, though he did not enjoy being 'gaped at like a wild beast' by them. To be fair to the local notables some of them encouraged visits to their houses by British officers. Bevan commented, a trifle cynically, that such visits had to be made 'to keep them in good humour'.

While he talked of there not being 'much progress in our acquaintance with the Spaniards', he did refer to his having one Spanish 'friend', namely the 'Minister' at Ceuta:

He speaks French very well, he has two sons, fine young men, and one daughter here who is pretty enough – his wife and another daughter have taken themselves to Gibraltar.[7]

From this glimpse it seems that Bevan had found a congenial and educated man with whom he could converse in French and so get to know. He appeared to regret that he had no Spanish, yet he made, like many of his race and caste, no effort to learn it.

For their part the British could, when needs must, give a good party for the Spaniards. The Commander-in-Chief, Gibraltar, had decreed that the occasion of King George III's birthday should be celebrated in as handsome a manner as possible. Accordingly the army at Ceuta responded in lavish style. Bevan wrote:

> The usual noise and confusion prevailed at this dinner [for 95 people], as at another of the same sort. The Spanish officers got amazingly drunk upon ale and port wine, to which they are but little used. In the evening a very select party of ladies consisting of Duchesses, Countesses and Marchionesses, such Devils! This I hear has given much offence to other families of the place, because they were not also invited. We had also a Bull Fight, salutes from the Batteries [and] an illumination at night! So much for the 4th June in Africa.[8]

After his first few letters home Bevan referred to the local population less frequently. When he did it was usually to comment along the lines of 'The Spaniards hate the sight of us, and I do not greatly wonder thereat, for we are English'. There is little doubt about Bevan's insularity!

He was also ungracious about English visitors to Ceuta from Gibraltar. Once a large party of English ladies was expected at Ceuta. He was hoping he would not see them, because they would be put off attempting the steep climb up to the citadel. As for the last set of visitors, he had given them 'some salt ham'. There must have been something nasty about it for he thought their account of the reception they had received at Ceuta and the ham they had had to eat would not induce others to follow in their footsteps (he was obviously wrong!). Nor had the English ladies compared favourably in his estimation with their Spanish counterparts, some of whom were 'nice looking and pretty'. At any rate, as he made it plain to Mary, the idea of entertaining people was not to his liking; it was 'as much as we can do to entertain ourselves'.[9] Charles may well have been prone to a little exaggeration for the sake of the story, but he hardly emerges as the most genial of hosts!

Certain subjects constantly exercise his mind: the vagaries of the mail; the changeable climate; the health problems of his men, especially the lingering effects of Walcheren fever and sometimes his own health, such as 'bile disorders', from which he apparently suffered (was he a bit of a hypochondriac?); his 'exile' or 'banishment' to Ceuta (he used both words), a posting which he came after a little time to hate, calling the place 'vile' and a 'dog-hole'; and the question of Colonel Wynch's promotion, a very favourite topic as he was desperately hoping this advancement would affect his own career and result in his leaving Ceuta.

Mary must have given Charles full rein for his complaints and niggles, judging by their uninhibited repetition, but he did at the same time enjoy the news from home, particularly about his boys, which Mary gave him faithfully and regularly. There is often charm in his injunctions and messages to his wife and children on whom he lavished much affection. Thus:

Pray how does little Charles get on in reading and speaking? I hope you will get the better of that terrible drawl, which is all habit, and a very bad habit. Believe me for once it is to be conquered.[10]

In early April came the news that Mary might be pregnant again. Charles wrote back by return:

I hope that you mistake the cause of your indisposition, but if you are right in your conjecture I pray to God you may in safety give to Mrs Shaw another little cousin. But I hope you are mistaken.[11]

She was right in her conjecture and henceforth until the autumn there were constant tender enquiries by the husband after his wife's well-being.

In his letters Charles often had a place for Mary's sister Eleanor, of whom he was very fond, and for Jim Paterson. To his evident pleasure the two were now married. Jim he described as an 'excellent hearted young man', even if he was to disappoint by his failure as a correspondent. At Ceuta, for instance, Charles was always hoping to hear from Jim, who, unaccompanied, arrived on a posting to Gibraltar in the summer. But Jim never wrote. Mary, we may recall, believed a soldier's wife's place was at her husband's side, home and abroad, a view not shared by Charles. On the decision that she should stay in England while he was in Ceuta he commented laconically, 'For once I did right'. He had by now seen through his eyes as a commanding officer the problems encountered by his soldiers' wives and women folk in Ceuta, where there were probably about twelve to a company. Another illustration of these sort of difficulties, if indeed one were needed, was provided by General Fraser himself, who could find no suitable accommodation in Ceuta for his wife and children, who perforce had to live in Gibraltar. The Rock, in Bevan's view, was no better place for families than Ceuta and he regaled Mary with the story of a friend, poor Mrs Mullins, the wife of Major Mullins of the 28th. She suffered innumerable tribulations through the illnesses of her children at Gibraltar, losing at least one child, as a result, we must presume, of the unfriendly climate and bad housing conditions. Her ultimate trial came later in the year when Major Mullins, on a rash British expedition to Malaga, was captured by the French and became a prisoner of war.

When his military life had begun to fall into a routine of a pretty humdrum nature, what did Bevan find to do? A search through the twenty-eight surviving letters he wrote to Mary during his eight-month sojourn in Ceuta is not very revealing. He did not shoot, nor was he adventurous enough to explore the hinterland of Ceuta or go to the old city of Tetuan in the south. He was not especially interested in his social life – the Mess was quite adequate for his needs. For exercise he rode, once his horse, labelled by him 'a melancholy creature', had arrived after no less than thirteen weeks on board ship – a long enough time to make any animal mope! On the other hand he enjoyed both receiving and writing letters, and the evidence suggests he was a good correspondent, responding keenly to those who wrote to him. Also reading was clearly a great solace to him. Then, as well as books, he loved poetry. Once, in a slightly morbid mood and reflecting on the idea of hope, he quoted from Oliver Goldsmith's *The Captivity*:

> Hope like a gleaming taper's light
> Adorns and cheers the way,
> And still as darker grows the night
> Emits a brighter ray[12]

On another occasion he quoted from *Hamlet* when expressing his 'love and friendship' to his sister-in-law Eleanor for being with Mary as the time for his wife's confinement approached.

There were for Bevan occasional visits to be made to Gibraltar on regimental business. Once he went to see if he could arrange some 'more active service' for his men to take the place of their seemingly perpetual garrison duties at Ceuta, though he met with no success, even if there was a measure of understanding from his superiors. While there he was better able to catch up on what was happening in Spain and Portugal, and would enjoy mulling over with like-minded men the progress of the war, his interest in which did not flag. Once on the Rock he found friends from the 28th there (the Light Company had done well in action at nearby Tarifa). On regimental news he was amused to hear that Colonel

Belson was contemplating matrimony. He also heard that Browne, ever a tough campaigning soldier, had been dangerously ill with Walcheren fever, but was recovering.

As Bevan sat and stagnated, as he saw it, at Ceuta in the summer of 1810 the situation in the Iberian peninsula did not look on the face of it too promising for the British. Lord Wellington, as Sir Arthur Wellesley had become after the Battle of Talavera, had beaten a tactical retreat back into Portugal towards the end of 1809, deciding to construct, secretly, the lines of Torres Vedras, as a defensive position between the Tagus and the Atlantic behind which his army could, and would, winter in security in future years. No significant reinforcements from England were at that moment forthcoming, so, biding his time, he would direct operations with effect from January 1810 from his headquarters at Viseu in the mountains in the middle of Portugal. In Spain the central Junta had abdicated at the end of January 1810 and soon afterwards King Joseph Bonaparte entered Seville. Except at Cadiz, open Spanish resistance to the French had collapsed, although the guerrilla war intensified and held down tens of thousands of French soldiers.

In May 1810 Napoleon appointed Marshal Andre Masséna, the 'old fox', to command the Army of Portugal , as it was called. The total number of French troops in Spain had now been raised to as many as 350,000, many of them fresh. Masséna lost no time in moving his forces towards central Portugal, his subordinate Ney capturing the Spanish fortress town of Ciudad Rodrigo in July, an event followed the next month by the surrender of the Portuguese fortress of Almeida, not far across the frontier. Almeida had been under the command of Colonel William Cox, though the troops of the garrison were mainly Portuguese. The French were fortunate to take the town, which is later on to assume an important place in our story, so easily and without having to besiege it. There are various accounts of what happened. According to Grehan, barrels of gunpowder were being loaded on to mules in the castle courtyard, to service the guns on the town walls. One barrel sprang a leak and consequently a trail of gunpowder led across the court-yard and through an open door to the main magazine. At this moment a random French shell landed in the castle setting fire to the trail which ran back and ignited the entire 150,000 lbs of stored gunpowder, as well as 1,000,000 cartridges. In the massive explosions and fires which followed hundreds of Portuguese soldiers and civilians died.[13] The historian Charles Oman called the disaster 'unparallelled in magnitude during the whole Peninsular War'.[14]

The progress of the French was being steadily observed by Wellington, now from Celorico. He had 33,000 British troops under him, and a Portuguese army, which, reorganized and retrained, was led by Marshal Beresford. Wellington was of course still very much in control of events. True, Masséna had invaded Portugal, but in September Wellington won a defensive battle against him at Busaco before retiring into the newly completed Lines of Torres Vedras. There he waited patiently until March before taking the offensive against the French.

Bevan was also biding his time, in his case rather impatiently, awaiting the promotion of Wynch. But as the summer of 1810, a hot uncomfortable one at Ceuta, dragged by there was, alas, no news on this, as he was constantly informing Mary. Another subject was sometimes raised by Bevan in his letters home. It was that of his 'Blue Devils', or, in other words, the deep depressions from which he sometimes suffered. A general cause for their onset seems to have been connected with his sense of isolation in Ceuta and his separation from Mary and his children. There were other influencing factors too, such as the boredom arising from an absence of active soldiering. Bevan had a brooding and introspective nature and, it would seem, had been prone to these depressions even before his marriage. It was to his wife, whom he always called his 'true friend', that he was accustomed to turn when the pressures of the world were almost too hard to bear. By midsummer he had been away from her for six months, not so long a time as in 1808/09 when, after service in Sweden, Portugal and finally Spain, he had been away for nine months, but the strain was beginning to show.

Sometimes news from home could trigger the onset of a depression. Once he told Mary that he was 'not in very good spirits today' as a result, it seems, of hearing that Mary was having difficulties in finding a suitable house. Another matter which preyed on his mind was whether the purchase of the lieutenant-colonelcy was a good or bad 'speculation'. He could not make up his mind on this abstract question. Yet he had to admit that if he had sold out of the army the previous year (as a major) they would never have had enough to live on.

One of his problems, when he was away from his family, and one he admitted to, was homesickness. He wrote in September, after some typical pessimistic ruminating, that 'I will not give you any more Blue Devils. But when I think of home I cannot help being somewhat melancholy'. On another occasion, in similar vein, he wrote that he wished that he was with her

> But, alas, it does not fall to my lot to feel much happiness. However I ought not to complain and will not. I have some things to be thankful for.[15]

In a more jocular mood he once confessed

> My mind is a little employed about my profession, which does not allow me so much time to entertain my friends the Blue Devils – not indeed that we have quite cut all connection and acquaintance but I am certainly not the miserable dog I sometimes used to be.[16]

But a reference in November to his 'evil destiny' pursuing him serves to show how his 'devils' continued to nag away at him in obsessive fashion.

It was not just the existence for Bevan of his obsessions, but it also weighed heavily with him that he had no one at hand in whom he could confide and share his innermost thoughts. At least he could spell out some of his worries to Mary in his letters, even though she was more than 1000 miles away. He once told her that, if he stayed in Ceuta much longer, 'I fear all my military spirit will evaporate'. On another occasion he said that he felt almost like a prisoner of war with nothing to vary 'the stale monotony of each succeeding day'.[17]

Poor Mary, at the receiving end of her husband's morbid fears and expressions of self-pity, must have felt anxious about him, however placid her temperament was, aware that if she had been at his side she would have helped dispel some of the gloom. This may explain why Mary was keen to accompany Charles overseas.

It would be wrong, however, to give the impression that Charles' outlook was always of the gloom and doom kind. It was not. When he was busy or campaigning he was a different man, for, of course, he did not have the time, or indeed the inclination, to indulge in unhealthy musings. Then he could sometimes produce some homespun philosophizing as in a letter written from Ceuta in late July:

How happy are those whom fortune has placed in a state of independence – but how equally often is that state abused, dispised and neglected – It is but by experience in life, and a knowledge of the world that one learns duly to appreciate the happiness of a calm and settled life – I believe therefore that a young man should always be employed in some active kind of life so that he may in his 'yellow leaf' know how to be satisfied with peace and friendship and a good wife.[18]

Not long after these reflections had been written Charles' peace of mind, always a fragile part of his psyche, suffered a rude shock. In August a letter from Mary brought some upsetting news. Mary had started by bringing excellent accounts of herself and the children before turning to give him some bad news about his sister, Julia. This is how Charles responded to his wife:

It is indeed necessary that I should have some good tidings to counterblanace that part of your letter which relates to my unfortunate Sister – Good God! Am I for ever destined to meet with such cruel strokes? Cruel I call them because after this most strange and unaccountable conduct how can I with sincerity look on her who ought to be one of my nearest and best friends in any light but in that of aversion – Ah! my dear Mary, God grant that you may never experience the sort of feeling I do at this moment – I can not help it, it is my nature – I had been a happier man was I born without some feelings. I possess – I mean, I hardly know what I mean – For I am so annoyed that my brain is quite in a whirl – How is all this to End? A pretty tale it all will be to be published all over the neighbourhood of Rickmansworth. I could not have well believed that one person however a stranger to me, could have been so utterly destitute of all honourable feeling, of all consideration for their family and after all that has happened before!!! My mother should have spoken out at least to her. Had I been in England I would have immediately have so done. But at this distance I ask what is left for me but to lament the disgrace that must fall not only where it should fall, but on all those connected with the party . . . I can not tell what to think about this casual affair; nor do I know how it is to terminate – I hope not in the way the Lady wills it – that in my opinion would be worse than any accident whatever.[19]

We must try and enlighten the reader as to what Julia had done. Unfortunately the precise facts are not known. As far as we can piece together the story from Charles' letters and from family information handed down, it seems that Julia, already a flirt, had formed an attachment with a man named Nevitt, who had probably given her singing lessons. At some stage Julia had eloped with Nevitt. We do not know if this was the first time she had left home for him or when exactly this elopement happened. Julia had then

100

returned home, apparently pregnant, but unmarried. However, it seemed that she still wanted to marry Nevitt. But Charles, we gather, was against a marriage. Whether he was at once aware of his sister's pregnancy is not clear.

The reaction shown by Charles to Julia's plight may seem harsh to us by today's standards, but was probably normal for the times. In his next letter to Mary he recognizes the 'confused' state of mind he had been in when composing his initial response, even if traces of self-pity are still only too evident. In course of time Charles' attitude to his errant sister changed and there was a softening in his initial unbending stance. Was this due all to Mary? By October Mrs Bevan and her two daughters had gone to live at Rottingdean in Sussex, probably with Mrs Walton, Charles' grandmother, and a month later Charles had a letter from Julia. He told Mary that he was 'glad to find she was in good spirits'. Thus a reconciliation between brother and sister, if this had indeed been needed, seemed to have taken place, and in a letter to Mary in December he sent via Mary his 'best love to my mother and sisters'. To jump still further ahead for a moment, in a not unsympathetic letter written at the end of February 1811 from Portugal, Charles thought:

> the neighbourhood of Chenies the last place on earth except Bedington that would have been selected. But I suspect there is more in this than meets the case . . . [I] know who takes a leading part in proposing these measures. Poor Julia I am sure would rather stay where she is.[20]

Chenies is a village a couple of miles north-west of Rickmansworth. Charles obviously believed that it would have been better for Julia to continue to stay at Rottingdean and have her child there. He seemed also to be blaming his mother for making what to him were unsatisfactory arrangements for Julia. Tragically Julia died young, either in childbirth or soon after her daughter was born. The child, also called Julia, was brought up by her spinster aunt Caroline.[21]

During his last few months in Ceuta Bevan's frustrations with the place continued to be evident. He saw his posting as being in a forgotten corner of the map, cut off both from military events and, more importantly, from Mary and news of her approaching confinement. Reinforcements to his still depleted battalion – some 150 men were due in Ceuta – had still not arrived (in June his full strength of fit soldiers was only 300). The condition of his men's health continued to be a constant preoccupation with him and, to his great regret, his second-in-command, Major Howard, died in September. Bevan commented to Mary that Howard 'never stirred out' and took little care of himself. Later to replace Howard, Major John Piper, a competent officer, was selected for a posting to Ceuta. Charles himself kept in good health, as he never tired of telling Mary. Whether the great quantity of medicine which he was accustomed to taking helped him is a matter for speculation. The army continued to suffer for a long time from Walcheren fever and at the end of the autumn there was a visitation at Gibraltar of some fever of an undisclosed nature, which, apart from its deadly effects, produced complications over quarantine for those like Bevan who travelled between Gibraltar and Ceuta.

Then, at long last, at the end of November Bevan received the two pieces of good news he had been waiting for. The first, relayed by his mother-in-law and Eleanor, was of the safe delivery to Mary of a daughter, Eleanor, named after her grandmother. The second was of Wynch's appointment to the staff. In an excited frame of mind, Bevan hurried off to Gibraltar almost as soon as he had these tidings. Never mind if he was not clear yet whether he was to be appointed to command the first battalion of the 4th, now in Portugal, or whether he would have the chance of making a visit to England. In fact, the answers to these queries turned out to be 'yes' to the first and 'no' to the second. But he could not wait to get to Portugal, though quarantine problems did not, we believe, allow him to return to Ceuta to make his farewells. No matter – he had loathed the place! So, in December he took passage in the first ship he could find going from Gibraltar to Lisbon. It proved to be a very dirty and uncomfortable Portuguese vessel, and he was charged, obviously he thought overcharged, £11 for the journey. He did not care. A new more vigorous chapter of his life, he hoped, was about to open.

CHAPTER NINE

The Line of Torres Vedras

Bevan stepped ashore on Portuguese soil for the second time late on 8 January 1811. The next day he wrote to Mary:

> After fifteen days passage from Gibraltar we anchored in the Tagus, when to our most unspeakable mortification we were put under quarantine where we remained eleven days, every hour expecting release; I came ashore last night and have been the whole morning occupied in arranging and in attending the funeral of poor Colonel Wynch, his death very sudden, in consequence of very violent fever. He had succeeded to the command of one of the Light Brigades of the army, in perfect health, happiness and spirits, expecting every day to be confirmed as Brigadier, he was Colonel on the staff; not quite so good a thing as to pay but in all other the same; Lord Wellington had given him this command in the most flattering manner. . . . I have not nor do I expect to see Paterson, but I have seen some of the 28th who tell me he is perfectly well and they never saw him so fat. He is on the other side of the river – This army is I understand, expecting strong reinforcements from home. . . . The moment I can procure some animal to carry my baggage and another to carry myself I am off to Torres Vedras where the battalion now is – a vast number of them are sick in Lisbon but I believe we can muster five or six hundred: and that is, I imagine, in this army a strong regiment.[1]

Wynch had died of a recurrence of Walcheren fever, his death serving as a reminder how that dreaded disease continued to haunt the army, even in Portugal. Captain Wood, the senior Captain of the 4th also died – cause undisclosed – two days after Bevan's arrival in Lisbon.

One of the first things Bevan did, once the two funerals were over, was to attend to his financial affairs. He needed funds to equip himself for the campaigning which lay ahead. One thing he did was to write to Hoare's bank in London to ensure that he could draw on money lying in the Bevan account. He was still in a muddle as to what the arrangements he had made at Hoare's were, for, as he told Mary:

> this is all owing to my stupidity in not recollecting whether we desired the money to be at your disposal, at mine or at both. Indeed I know it is at yours, but I do not remember if it is at mine.[2]

In dealing with these matters Bevan could not resist comparing his state with that of the 'Mantua apothecary' in *Romeo and Juliet*, the disorder from which that character suffered being his poverty!

Soon, Bevan met his brother-in-law, Jim Paterson, who had left England early the previous summer to join the 28th abroad. By the time Charles arrived in Portugal Paterson was with the second battalion east of the Tagus. He had of course seen Charles' family more recently than Charles himself and would have been receiving letters from his wife Eleanor, who, like her sister Mary, was living with her mother at Rickmansworth. The two men, therefore, would have a lot of family news to discuss. There was one particular and rather sensitive matter mentioned by Jim to Charles. This related to what Charles had been telling Mary for a long time, namely how he had high hopes of taking over the First Battalion from Wynch. The Battalion was stationed in Essex until November 1810, when it left for service in Portugal. Up to that date Bevan had visualized returning home for the hand-over, when

105

he would see his family. He had also, while at Ceuta, specifically told Mary that 'I shall get leave of absence and I hope before the expiration of that leave he [Wynch] must get something'.[3] All this must have been music to Mary's ears and she must have set great store by the prospect of Charles coming home. But he did not come and did not come. Perhaps in all this she forgot Charles' habit of sometimes indulging in a favourite pastime, that of building castles in the air.

No doubt Mary confided to her sister her disappointment that her expectations were never realized. Probably she was a bit critical of Charles, though never disloyal. Now all this, as seen through the eyes of Eleanor, was being relayed in Lisbon by Jim to Charles, who was clearly a trifle dismayed to hear how Mary had been feeling. At any rate he at once wrote to Mary, expecting, as he told her, 'your jobation', in other words a scolding. This did not stop him from saying to her that he did not 'want it to be said that I told you that we were coming home'.[4] Of course he should have realized that Mary would have no secrets from Eleanor and that there was a danger of Charles' views on the succession to Wynch being noised abroad. So Charles and Mary seemed to have been a little at cross-purposes, but, whatever this amounted to, there is no further reflection on this matter in further correspondence.

To be fair to Charles, there had been uncertainties about the army's position in the Iberian peninsula, and therefore in Ceuta, for some time. These really stemmed from King George III's physical disabilities, arising from what was seen in those days as his 'madness', but which we now understand to have been the result of his suffering from porphyria. The Regency Bill was not passed until February 1811, and before its passage there was much speculation that the Prince Regent would turn, on his acquiring certain constitutional powers, towards the Whigs under Lord Grenville to form a government. In this contingency the Whigs, it was widely considered, and Lord Wellington was of this view, would try and end the war with France. This would mean the army, or at least most of it, returning home. It is not so surprising in these circumstances that army officers in Portugal, including Bevan, were infected with the bug of uncertainty about their future. This could, for instance, account for him ending a letter written to Mary as late as 15 January: 'I hope soon to embrace you and our children'.

In the event the Prince proved to be indecisive about committing himself to the Whigs,[5] or he may have been cautious while there was hope of the King's recovery. Consulted by him, the doctors thought that the King might indeed get better within some months. In any case Grenville was not too keen for office and did not push for it. So the Prince decided to continue with the Tory Perceval as Prime Minister and to maintain the war against France. By February there was no more talk by Bevan in his letters to Mary of any hopes of his being home soon.

He was only in Lisbon for a week or so, but he quickly decided that he disliked the place, describing it as filthy and crowded with refugees from the war, both from Spain and from up-country Portugal. He was not alone in his views of Lisbon which was described by a sergeant as a 'dung hill from end to end' . He had plenty to do, both regimental and personal business, and admitted to Mary that he was 'so hurried and bothered that I hardly have time to write to you'. He did not like it that the Regiment had been, as he put it, 'poked away' in the 5th Division and brigaded with the unseasoned men of the 30th (Cambridgeshire) and 44th (East Essex) regiments. The Division was commanded by Major-General James Leith, and the Brigade by Major-General James Dunlop, of whom Bevan seemed a trifle critical because he wore 'green spectacles'!

Leith had in fact been bickering rather childishly with General Picton on the subject of whose division had saved the day at the Battle of Busaco the previous year, only to fall ill with a recurrence of Walcheren fever. Wellington was apparently not sorry, one of his biographers suggests, to let him go home on sick leave.[6] Nevertheless, Leith was popular in the Division, who regretted his departure. As it was, Leith's temporary disappearance from the

Peninsular War was to have momentous consequences for Bevan, because the disastrous Sir William Erskine soon came to be appointed to command the 5th Division for a short but critical time. There will be more about Erskine in due course.

Bevan arrived at the town of Torres Vedras in the middle of January and was there until the army moved off in March to chase the French from Portugal. His arrival coincided with the return of bad weather and the men's consequent relapse into sickness. He reported to Mary at the end of the month that 'I have not yet got quite settled with my new corps and it must be sometime before I can feel quite at home'. A few days later he repeated this, adding that it was a 'great bore to be making new acquaintances every day of your life.'[7] Here again was that slightly anti-social streak in Bevan resurfacing. Nevertheless, it is not surprising that the new commanding officer took a little while to shake down. What of course he wanted was action and this took a few weeks to come.

The Lines of Torres Vedras had been conceived by Wellington in the autumn of 1809 as a defensive measure and had then taken a year to build. Thus they had not been occupied by the army until October 1810, after the Battle of Busaco had been fought. Wellington had given his very able chief sapper, Lieutenant-Colonel Richard Fletcher, a twenty-one point memorandum laying down his requirements for the Lines. He then left Fletcher and his men to get on with the works without interference. In fact only once during the Lines' construction did Wellington inspect the progress made, such was his confidence in Fletcher's ability. There were two principal lines of fortifications, with a short third one, which was designed to cover any emergency embarkation, near the mouth of the Tagus. In all a chain of fifty-nine redoubts or forts, excluding advanced posts, were built by a labour force of between 5000 and 7000 men,[8] through the hilly country covering 52 miles. The fortifications were served by 232 pieces of artillery secured in the redoubts, which were connected by a network of interior roads to allow for the quick movement of troops and equipment. A hill-top system of semaphore stations enabled messages to travel from one end of the Lines to the other in just seven minutes. The plan was for the forts to be manned by second-line troops, while the main echelons of the army were concentrated behind them ready for rapid deployment to whatever position came under enemy threat.

The construction of the Lines was a huge achievment, even though they were never tested in battle, for they effectively sealed off the Lisbon peninsula from the country to the north, with the sea on one side and the Tagus on the other. Wellington, wanting to make life as difficult for Masséna as possible, tried to get the Portuguese government to introduce a scorched earth policy north and east of the Lines so that there would be no food or fodder for the French army and their horses. In this he was only partially successful, but where he was just about wholly successful was in maintaining secrecy over the building of the Lines. Neither the British government nor the Portuguese Regency Council nor, most importantly, the French army were really aware of what Wellington had been doing. When Masséna first saw the Lines as he recce'd in front of them he was convinced that they were impregnable and that they were not worth attacking. At first he may have hoped the British would leave their fastness and do battle with him in the open. But Wellington was never tempted to do so and after a month Masséna withdrew his Army of Portugal to defensive positions centred on Santarem, reporting to Napoleon that further progress would be impossible without reinforce-ments. In the meantime Masséna found some consolation in the company of his 18-year-old mistress, Henriette Leberton, who liked to dress as a Hussar with tight-fitting breeches and furlined pelisse.[9]

By the end of the winter, with starvation staring his army in the face, Masséna finally decided to withdraw and return with his men to Spain. Wellington had been vindicated in his belief that the Lines would act as a security bastion in the winter months, behind which his forces could recuperate and regroup without hindrance.

In early 1811 Bevan wielded a busy pen. Torres Vedras, he told Mary, was situated in a 'nasty hollow' filled with 'swamp'. Surprisingly, he ventured no comment on the Lines beyond saying the summits of the hills were 'strongly fortified'. He did not go into a lot of detail about his men and their lives, but did refer to his worries concerning their health and also their footwear. The British Army seems for ever to have had trouble with its boots! If the minutiae of his regimental life was not always revealed to Mary, he did often display in letters considerable interest in the wider military/political picture; for instance future campaigning prospects for the army and the political scene at home. In the middle of February he was writing to Mary indicating how much he enjoyed a sight of newspapers from home:

> The debates of our Parliament are just now very interesting and I like to pore over them. I would not make this request [for papers to be sent out] was it attended with the slightest difficulty of expense.[10]

Was this an occupation one would expect of a run-of-the-mill soldier during his leisure time? Hardly. This and occasional similar references make me wonder whether Bevan, had he had private means, might not have found politics an attractive career to follow.

As ill-luck would have it, one of Bevan's two baggage mules was kicked by his horse and died, requiring him to buy another one. This led him to complain that he had 'no horse fit for travelling – in short I am very badly equipped in all ways'. With him things tended to be right or wrong; rarely was there a half-way position! At least he was well-housed and said so:

> I have at last got a tolerable good quarter which had been previously occupied by General Dunlop, but who quitted it in consequence of its being flooded whenever the rain sets in which is just now the case – I have one half of the house and

110

a Colonel McMahon the other. We are not acquainted. The General had built a fire place which I find a most delectable treat in this very damp weather. We are very well off for things to eat and for those who have plenty of money there is no scarcity of port wine to drink but it is as dear as in England; it will not therefore suit my finances at present.[11]

While the French were desperately short of food, as Wellington meant them to be, the British, especially those on the banks of the Tagus, were well supplied, although distribution of the food, as Bevan observed, could be something of a problem.

The state of the local people, often as a direct result of the scorched earth policy, caused Bevan some concern, and he compared scenes he witnessed with what Oliver Goldsmith, a favourite poet of his, described in his poem *The Deserted Village*, written forty-one years earlier:

One can not behold entire families of all ages and sexes . . .
helpless and almost naked to the mercy of the winter wind
without almost becoming a philosopher and shuddering at
the horror of war.[12]

'We were,' he went on, 'last night blessed with a slight touch of an earthquake,' which had involved the 'shaking' of his house. All this alarmed the local people, as well it might have. By an odd coincidence Bevan had just been reading, before he went to bed, about the great earthquake of 1755, which almost totally destroyed Lisbon. He had mentioned this recent tremor in case Mary read about it and was 'unnecessarily alarmed'.

This narrative has at times shown there to have been certain failings in Bevan's character, such as a tendency to indulge in self-pity. He sometimes recognized his own shortcomings as when he wrote to Mary in somewhat introspective mood, although what precisely prompted him to make these remarks is not clear from the context:

I know I am very often most particularly disagreeable and I am quite aware that unluckily I cannot change my nature – I suppose with me it is constitutional – for I am very often exceedingly otherwise than agreeable to myself. I hope your little sons will not inherit their father's failings.[13]

In justice to Bevan, we do perhaps need to balance those occasions which show his character in a poor light with ones from which he emerges with credit. For instance, when Mary wrote to tell him of Edward being ill he wrote back with compassion even if the effect is slightly spoiled by the last sentences:

I have just received, my dearest Mary, your unfinished account of our poor little boy's illness; I trust that the doctors expectations will be fulfilled and the poor little sufferer be restored to the tender attention of his excellent mother. But I confess to you that my chief anxiety is on your own account, the favourable turn in Edward's case I hope leaves no fear of relapse, but the fatigue and anxiety you have so constantly sustained makes me tremble for you. I conjure you to take some care of yourself, and to recollect that you are by no means the strongest person in the world. You are fortunately in the midst of your own family who I well know will take every possible care of you and advise you in your labour as much as you will allow them to do. If it was not for this I should never have a moment's peace. God knows those moments of ease are not too frequent with me.[14]

When Charles got a bunch of letters from Mary at the end of February written in January he was much comforted by the 'good news of our dear little people' and to hear that Edward was almost restored to full health. There was also a gentle admonition to his wife that he had wanted to hear how 'Mrs C Bevan does because in your three letters there is not one word of her and as she is a tolerably good sort of person I wish particularly [to know] the state of her health'. Here he is, of course, referring to Mary.

He took enormous delight in having news of the doings of his sons and nowhere is there a better example of this than in his comments about the following little ceremony. Charles, aged five, had shown, Mary recounted, anxiety and fear about putting on the 'manly habit'. This was the occasion – rather a ritual – when a small boy in those days left his baby clothes behind him to don proper boy's clothes with breeches, etc. Evidently children were sometimes loath to make the change and Charles was full of sympathy for his son's reluctance to accept his breeches. 'I have the most perfect remembrance of my own feelings over that interesting occasion,' wrote the father, 'as well as of the telling a most tremendous lie which delayed the accomplishment of my wishes for three days. I hope some day or other I may be permitted to share with you the happiness of these moments.'

While Charles' love for his family was a very genuine one, and was often charmingly expressed to Mary, free of all inhibitions, it is not easy to make out the real nature of his relationship with his mother and sisters. He and his mother seem to have corresponded only intermittently, and at the end of February, on learning from Mary that his mother and sisters were moving house to near Rickmansworth, he expressed a 'good deal' of astonishment. Rather pathetically, he commented that, as he had never heard from any member of the family about it, he supposed 'they no longer consider me as belonging to them.' There can be little doubt that Charles had neither love nor respect for his mother. There is no obvious explanation for this except that the strong impression gained from Charles' letters – he himself does not quite say this – is that she was a silly, even irresponsible, woman who showed little interest in her son, daughter-in-law or their young family.

Life for Bevan underwent a dramatic change at the end of the first week in March. A peasant came into the British outposts opposite Santarem about 20 miles north of the Lines with the news that the French had decamped in the night leaving their watch-fires burning.[15] The Peninsular War was like a see-saw. One minute the French attacked and the allies retired. The next moment the roles were reversed. Now, quite suddenly, it was the turn of the French to retreat and of the allies to advance.

CHAPTER TEN

From the Tagus to the Côa

The French army, anchored at Santarem, had suffered grievously during the winter of 1810/11 and were only kept in place by Masséna's iron resolve that his forces should stay close to Lisbon. Desperately short of food and prone to disease, their numbers had been dwindling in the inimical Portuguese environment. Sixty-five thousand men had crossed into Portugal by mid-September 1810. Three and a half months later these numbers were down to 46,500, though in January the army was reinforced by 7,600 men. Moreover, they had lost 5,800 horses out of 14,000 brought into the country, mostly eaten.[1] Isolated from Spain, their rear was subject to constant harrying by local militia and guerrillas. Stragglers were likely to be murdered. It was hardly surprising that in these circumstances, and with morale in the army low, Masséna decided he had no option but to retreat. In the meantime Wellington had been waiting for reinforcements. When these finally arrived, he began to form a 7th Division.

Despite a reconnaissance of the French position at Santarem on 5 March, the British were taken by surprise when Masséna made his move to withdraw that evening. Thus the French gained twenty-four precious hours over their enemy. Masséna's initial intention was to fall back through the coastal plain to the Mondego River and then if necessary to go back still further in the direction of Oporto.[2]

The British pursuit was at first a cautious one. When Wellington realized that Masséna's retreat was on a major scale he

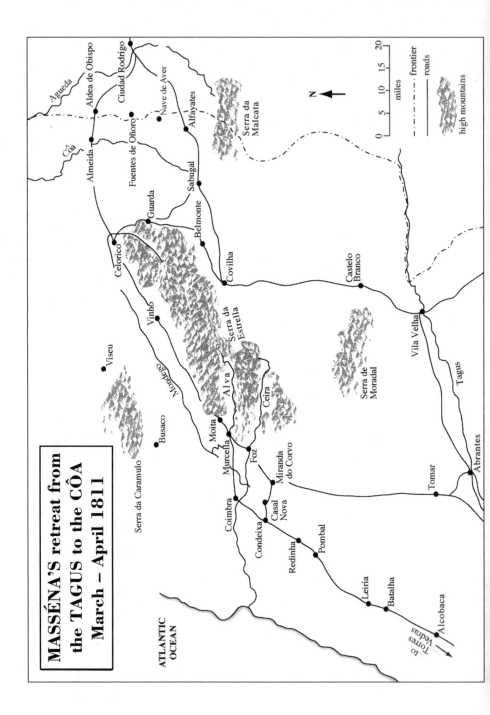

MASSÉNA'S retreat from
the TAGUS to the CÔA
March – April 1811

ATLANTIC
OCEAN

The landing of British troops in Egypt, March 1801 (engraving of a painting by de Loutherbourg).   *(National Army Museum)*

The 28th Regiment at the Battle of Alexandria, 21 March 1801.
                                        (Soldiers of Gloucestershire Museum)

3. An engraving of Ceuta in 1572. *(The British Historical Society of Portugal)*

Lieutenant General Sir John Moore (painting by Sir Thomas Lawrence c.1805).

5. Major General Sir William Erskine Bt (mezzotint by S.W. Reynolds after Richard Cosway). *(National Army Museum)*

General Sir Edward Paget. *(Soldiers of Gloucestershire Museum)*

7. The Duke of Wellington (painting by P. E. Stroehling c.1815). *(National Army Museum)*

8. Almeida: a gateway today. (W. Colfer)

IV

LIEUT COL CHARLES BEVAN, 4ᵗʰ OR KING'S OWN REGT
THIS STONE IS ERECTED TO THE MEMORY
OF CHARLES BEVAN, LATE LIEUT.
COL. OF THE 4ᵗʰ OR KINGS OWN REGT, WITH
THE INTENTION OF RECORDING HIS
VIRTUES. THEY ARE DEEPLY ENGRAVEN ON THE
HEARTS OF THOSE WHO KNEW HIM
AND WILL EVER LIVE IN THEIR REMEMBRANCE.

A STONE WITH THIS INSCRIPTION WAS
ERECTED OVER THE GRAVE OF COL
BEVAN IN PORTALEGRE CASTLE WHERE HE WAS
BURIED ON 11 JULY 1811. THAT
STONE HAVING BEEN REMOVED WHEN A ROAD
WAS BUILT THERE, THIS REPLACEMENT
IS PLACED BY HIS DESCENDANTS TO HONOUR THE
MEMORY OF AN OFFICER WHO PUT
REGIMENTAL HONOUR BEFORE HIS OWN LIFE.
ERECTED ON BEHALF OF ANN COLFER
(D 1980) AND SARA CAVALEIRO, DAUGHTERS
OF MAJOR JAMES BEVAN WHO
CARRIED CHARLES SWORD DURING HIS OWN
SERVICE IN THE KING'S OWN 1913-1935
AND OF MRS. R. STAFFORD, HUGH STAFFORD,
MARGARET SMITH AND DIANA
THOMAS AND THEIR CHILDREN.

WILLIAM COLFER CB, 14 OCTOBER 2000

9. The stone at Elvas cemetery, Portugal, which was dedicated to the memory of Charles Bevan in October 2000. *(W. Colfer)*

threw the bulk of his army, six divisions in all, after the enemy. Bevan's regiment, still in the 5th Division, now commanded by Dunlop, formed part of this force, though was not in its vanguard. It was not until 11 March that the leading elements of the Anglo-Portuguese army in the shape of the cavalry and of the Light Division, now under the temporary command of Sir William Erskine in the absence of that strict disciplinarian 'Black Bob' Craufurd who was on leave, caught up with Ney's rearguard at Pombal. Here, it is said, Erskine handled his division 'clumsily'.[3] For a moment it looked as if the French would make a stand, but instead their retreat continued some miles on to Redinha where heavy skirmishing took place.

The road north, as Bevan witnessed, was not a pretty sight. General Picton, in command of the 3rd Division and a hardened soldier, wrote that nothing could exceed the 'devastation and cruelties committed by the enemy during his retreat . . . for leagues on each Flank of his march'[4.] Captain Kincaid of the greenjacketed 95th, hard on the heels of the French, described Santarem as looking like the city of the plague, while in another small town:

> young women were lying in their houses brutally violated – the streets were strewn with broken furniture, intermixed with the putrid carcases, murdered peasants, mules and donkeys and every description of filth, that filled the air with pestilential nausea. The few starved male inhabitants who were stalking amid the wreck of their friends and property looked like so many skeletons.[5]

The French had put the old town of Leiria to the torch and, in their spite, had ransacked the famous monasteries of Alcobaca and Batalha, the former being burnt on the express orders of French headquarters.[6]

Wellington's tactics of pressing closely after his enemy and giving them no respite began to pay off. He skilfully manoeuvered

Ney's rearguard out of the important road junction town of Condeixa. Colonel Trant, to the north and on guard with six battalions of militia, bravely prevented the French from attempting to cross the Mondego and in so doing contributed to the saving of the beautiful city of Coimbra from the depredations of the French. As he was swept north-eastwards on the road to Celorico and towards the mountains, Masséna saw that he would now have to consider a retreat back to the Spanish border and Ciudad Rodrigo.

At the village of Casal Nova there came on 14 March a bad moment for the British. Erskine, concluding in error that the French were in full retreat, 'rashly and with astounding indifference', in the words of the historian William Napier, sent the tough 52nd regiment (Oxfordshire) of the Light Division rushing after the enemy in thick mist. This regiment soon found itself isolated and, worse, in the middle of the French position. As a result the rest of the division had to go to its assistance.[7] Both William Napier and his brother George, of the 52nd, were wounded in the affair. Indeed George described Erskine's recklessness in frank and revealing terms. When told by a colonel that the French were still in possession of Casal Nova, Erskine 'kept blustering and swearing it was all nonsense – that the captains of the pickets knew nothing about the matter and that there was not a man in the village'. As Erskine spoke the fog began to clear and there came from the direction of the village a regular cannonade of enemy gunfire, showing just how wrong he had been.[8]

Shortly after this engagement Masséna decided to abandon all non-essential wagons and the army's baggage. British soldiers, as they reached Miranda do Corvo, and the wild and hilly countryside surrounding it, saw to their horror the full results of this decision, for he had also ordered the hamstringing of as many as 500 pack animals, horses, mules and donkeys, all of whom had been left to die in torment. Most of these ill-fed animals were skin and bone and would in any case have been useless to the British.

The last full rearguard action in this phase of the French retreat was fought on 15 March at Foz do Arouce, where Ney left three brigades on the allied side of the River Ceira. Picton and Erskine believed it was too late in the day to attack, but just before dusk Wellington came up and saw that few of the enemy were under arms. He therefore immediately ordered an attack which caused the surprised French to fall back in confusion. After this minor setback their retreat continued at a steady speed until Celorico, a town situated at the northern end of the Estrella mountain range, was reached. Here on 21 March Masséna halted, having succeeded in putting his men several days' march ahead of the British, who had outrun their supply trains. Some days earlier Wellington had detached the 2nd and 4th Divisions under Beresford with the object of relieving Badajoz (this was before news of its surrender to the French came through). With this force went Paterson and the 28th Foot, whose progress thereafter Bevan keenly followed as far as he was able.

As at Casal Nova, the 5th Division, and so Bevan's 4th Foot, were not involved in the action at Foz as they had still been bringing up the rear. After Foz Wellington sent the 5th Division up a steep road into the mountains along the top of a ridge to cross the upper waters of the Alva River and to try and turn the French position. The result was that the French were forced to retire to another ridge.[9] Eventually the Division rejoined the main road at Moita, where it halted for a few days to await supplies. Bevan, on campaign, was as faithful a correspondent as time allowed. On the march his letters were maybe a little less polished than the ones he wrote from the comfort of more permanent quarters. He now took advantage of this breather to write to Mary quite chattily:

I have just heard that an opportunity of sending letters to England offers itself and therefore I avail myself of a drum-head to tell you that we are in close pursuit of Marshal Masséna. Lord Wellington has been in close Rear Guard as the country through which we are ever marching is remarkably thorny, consequently being favourable for his defence. I do not know the name of the place where we are at this moment, or I judge it has none as there is not a house in the vicinity. The French have been completely foiled in two attempts to cross the Mondego River, in one instance at the Bridge of Coimbra, in the second at the Bridge of Murcella higher up. It has fallen almost literally to the lot of the Light Division to force the Enemy from his positions which has been always effected though with some loss; it is imagined theirs is more considerable than ours. You may consider me as safe as if at Money Hill. We, however, [have] plenty of Fatigue and the weather has become wet which for Night Marches is not delightful. You will be glad to hear I am perfectly well. But very [illegible] for horses which in this incessant marching is very inconvenient. Lord W. has certainly saved the Town of Coimbra from devastation. The French have entirely destroyed by fire every Town, Village through which they have passed; the beautiful one of Leiria with its famous Cathedral is just in the same state as the Theatre of Drury Lane after the fire. The acts of barbarian atrocity they exercise above the unfortunate people would disgrace the annals of the Goths. They [are] literally wanton in savage inhumanity. If they will fight us they will be properly punished, but I am afraid they are too clever to be compelled to do so, having the advantage of a start. We have [been] marching something like that to Corunna, but we are now the chase. Paterson's Brigade is on the other bank of the Tagus at which he perhaps is mortified; but very likely they will [get] their share in that quarter. I have only time to say to you God Bless you and all yours. I am much hurried but you know always yours. C.B.

I hope to get a bit of red ribbon for my button hole.[10]

As both armies paused, Masséna contemplated what he should now do. Unhappy at the prospect of recrossing the same border by which he had entered Portugal and wishing no doubt to save face, he decided quite unexpectedly to countermarch to the lofty town of Guarda, some ten miles to his south, then make for Sabugal before taking up an entirely new position in the distant Coria-Plasencia area of Spain. In this way, he felt, he would open up communications with Marshal Soult at Badajoz. Subsequently the combined forces of the two marshals, so he argued, might pose a renewed threat to central Portugal, but this time from the east. This ill-thought-out scheme found no favour with Ney. Denied support, Masséna at once deprived his subordinate of his command and sent him back to Paris. In the event Masséna's plan, also disliked by Junot and Reynier, came unstuck. Realizing that there would be an absence of lateral roads and that the problem of finding food both en route to and in the Plasencia area would be a massive one, Masséna finally saw that he could not carry through his design. By the beginning of April he therefore aborted his plan and the French took up a position defending a line of over 20 miles on the River Côa, one of a series of rivers flowing south to north and debouching eventually into the Douro. Reynier held the left of the front in the bend of the river at Sabugal, a small walled town with a Moorish castle, while Junot was 10 miles behind at Alfayates. On the far right the French 9th corps was stationed near Almeida.

Still engaged in the pursuit of the French, Bevan managed to get letters off to Mary on 27 and 30 March. The first, taking amazingly enough only two and a half weeks to reach England from a remote spot on the hills of central Portugal, was a shortish one with little real news:

After a very long and difficult day's march I have, however, just strength and power to keep my eyes open to send you a few lines. I am quite well. This army continues to follow up the movements of the enemy. . . . we have made several prisoners and taken some guns, I am not quite sure of the numbers of either. It is very fatiguing as we get little rest and little to eat and drink. The name of the village we have just come to is Vinho; but of which there is a plentiful scarcity. . . . If anybody would give me enough to live in the country with you I believe I should be tempted by it . . . the scenes of misery we are daily witness to is quite beyond expression. . . . I have not been in a house till today these three weeks almost.[11]

His comment on the lack of food was a fair one. Brigadier-General Denis Pack, commanding a Portuguese brigade, referred in his memoirs to 'the bad commissariat and worse medical establishment' at this time. Captain Kincaid, also seeking food at this point in the campaign, came across some nuns in a mountain village. They had fled from a convent and were waiting outside an oven for some 'Indian corn-leaven' to be baked. He explained his pressing wants and two of them generously gave him a share of their food. 'I gave each a kiss and a dollar between; they took the former as an unusual favour; but looked at the latter inasmuch as to say "Our poverty, and not our will, consents." I ran off with my half-baked dough, and joined my comrades.'[12]

Bevan's letter of 30 March was full of information about the behaviour of the enemy:

We are now resting, but I know not for how long a period in a small village named Porco, most applicable indeed to the nastiness of the place. In a most beautiful valley under the high ground on which stands the city of Guarda, about 5 miles distant, the French left that place yesterday and whenever their route is exactly ascertained we shall I imagine follow; most likely this day, for 24 hours is a long rest in our present state. They have not succeeded in burning Guarda, although they had set it on fire, some people were too quick upon them, but they have left it in so filthy a state that it is impossible to describe. The people would actually blush to bear witness to such nastiness. There are or rather have been

122

some very charming houses in this valley, the property of rich people, the French have burned them all. The poor servants who were left in charge of these country residences had buried various articles of their masters' property such as china etc, very valuable, in and about the gardens belonging to these places; but the cunning of the French was superior to this for whenever they observed, and they took pretty good care to examine, the earth newly turned, they probed with thin ramrods, or other equally searching instruments until they discovered the hidden goods and what they could not carry away or did not want, they broke in a thousand pieces & left them for us. The horrid cruelties they committed are too shocking to relate but it is not by order of their officers. On the contrary, I have been told by the French soldiers themselves that they are stricly forbidden to murder but the burning of the Towns etc is an order of Masséna. Whenever the Portuguese catch any of these prisoners without an English escort they wreak a bitter vengeance upon them. I have not heard from Paterson, but I imagine they will have enough to do in their neighbourhood. We are very hardly off for eating and drinking and are not likely to be better for some time.

We expect to move into Guarda but most likely shall not remain there more than a day, at least I hope so for it is the worst [illegible] in the country and now perfectly deserted. The poor 4th have left behind on this march one hundred men. So you may imagine we are a little pushed. Out of eight hundred men we have only five hundred and twenty now at Porco. General Hay has this moment called to tell me we march tomorrow morning and I trust to God do not remain at Guarda but march through it after a Corps of about 7,600 French who are marching towards Belmonte. But I am afraid they have too much the start of us. I must now go and prepare my family for getting under weigh (sic) . . . My boys are full as troublesome to keep in any order as yours can be. I wish I

would be so pleased as only to think and attend to **our own**
[Bevan's emphasis] instead of the King's Own! But that is
. . . foolish and therefore I must do the best I can to attend to
both . . . I hope I shall be finished ere very long to be among
you.[13]

The expulsion of the French from Portugal being his principal
aim, Wellington moved his forces south-eastwards to confront
Reynier's 2nd Corps at Sabugal. His plan was to turn the French
left using the Light Division and the cavalry, and thereby to sever
the enemy's line of retreat. He felt he might, if successful, inflict
a damaging defeat on Reynier. The 5th Division was on the British
left and was directed to force the bridge across the Côa at Sabugal.
This gave Bevan the promise of real action at last. But it was not
to be . . .

Once again Erskine came to the rescue of the enemy. On 3 April,
the day planned for the allied attack, a dense fog descended over
the Sabugal area. Picton and Dunlop, commanding the 3rd and
5th Divisions respectively, decided, prudently enough in the
circumstances, to stay their hands. Not so the rash Erskine, who
precisely repeated the mistake he had made twenty days earlier at
Casal Nova. Not bothering to take any steps to find out about the
lie of the land or where the enemy might be, he simply told an
ADC to order the Light Division to descend to the river, ford it
and press on. The inevitable happened. In the fog the correct ford
was missed by Beckwith's brigade and, instead of crossing two and
a quarter miles up stream from Sabugal, the troops crossed only
one mile from the town. As a consequence Beckwith's 1,500 men
found themselves confronting two French divisions in a good
defensive position. A mighty fight now raged. In the meantime,
becoming cautious, Erskine forbade the brigade following under
Drummond to cross the Côa. But, hearing heavy firing from the
direction Beckwith had taken, Drummond, ignoring orders,
hastened to the sound of the guns. In the event the Light Division

was only able to extricate itself from a tight corner with some difficulty, though with much gallantry. No thanks, however, to Erskine. As for the cavalry, whose role was important, in the words of Oman, 'Erskine contrived to make them useless, counter-marching in the mist some way from the fighting front'.[14] While the 5th Division achieved their objective in this action without losing a man, they played no part in the main battle and were too far on the left to be of any use in the pursuit, the execution of which had anyhow been bungled. So while the French were defeated at Sabugal, losing some 700 men, Wellington's bold plan of destroying Reynier's corps was frustrated. Nevertheless, as the French line on the Côa was broken the way to the frontier was now open to Wellington.

A few days after Sabugal Erskine was in command of an operation mounted by Wellington to clear the French 9th corps from the Almeida area. According to Oman the General's military competency was again found wanting, though less seriously perhaps than his failures at Casal Nova and Sabugal. This time he merely failed to use the opportunity to press home an advantage gained over the retreating French after a promising attack by the dragoons.[15] As a commander on the battlefield, nothing seemed to go right for the man.

Erskine's role in the later part of Bevan's story is a fairly crucial one and we must take therefore a closer look at this contentious figure. A Scot from Fifeshire, he was born in 1770, the son of a general who had served in nineteen campaigns. While a Captain in the 15th Light Dragoon Guards he had distinguished himself by his gallantry while serving in Flanders at the start of the French revolutionary wars. In 1795 he succeeded to his father's baronetcy and considerable income and a year later became MP for Fifeshire. Unhappily, he was unstable and prone to bouts of insanity; once, it is said, he was incarcerated in an asylum. When Wellington heard that Erskine was to be posted to Portugal, he remonstrated that he had 'generally understood him to be a madman'. Horse

Guards[16] replied: 'No doubt he is sometimes a little mad but in his lucid intervals he is an uncommonly clever fellow; and I trust he will have no fit during the campaign, though he looked a little wild as he embarked'. Robert Long, a fellow cavalry general in the Peninsular War, also thought Erskine was mad. He seems, as well, to have acquired the reputation of being a heavy drinker. Writing in the 1920s Huddlestone, once the Librarian in the War Office, put it that Erskine 'was not unacquainted with the Demon Rum'. Elizabeth Longford, in her biography of Wellington, does not mince her words when she described Erskine as an 'unstable, dim-eyed drunkard'. By 'dim-eyed' she was referring to his chronic short-sightedness which caused him to wear spectacles, something of an encumbrance for a cavalry commander. The optimistic expectations of Horse Guards proved to be ill-founded, for at some stage during his career with Wellington, it was reported that Erskine had to be sent home 'indisposed'. Nevertheless he made some kind of a comeback and was even promoted to the local rank of Lieutenant-General. But a tragic end was in store for him. Having left the army, he stayed on in Portugal and in May 1813, while living in Lisbon, he threw himself to his death from an upstairs window.[17]

One man, the historian S.G.P. Ward, has, however, gamely defended Erskine's undistinguished reputation. In Ward's eyes, Erskine had been ill used. While admitting that he was 'highly strung', no one, Ward stated, could exceed this aimable man in his anxiety to do the right thing. Nevertheless, Ward had to agree that 'officers dreaded serving under him in action' and that his performance under the stress of active war seems gradually 'to have deteriorated with (or in spite of) his practice of taking stimulants.'[18] Ward does comment on Erskine's military capabilities.

This then was the man who in 1811 was one of Wellington's divisional commanders, a man most commentators believe to have been without military aptitude and to have often shown carelessness over the lives of the men under his command. So it is surprising that this soldier, of whom Wellington eventually said no reliance could be placed on his judgement, continued for so long to hold senior posts in the army in the Peninsula. No doubt it demonstrated the power of Horse Guards, but it certainly did not reflect well upon Wellington himself.

CHAPTER ELEVEN

Almeida: Relief Foiled

After the battle of Sabugal Masséna's forces retreated over the border into Spain, with the exception of the garrison under General Antoine Brenier left behind to defend the fortress town of Almeida. Masséna's incursion into Portugal had cost him, in a seven-month period, 25,000 men, of whom a quarter were prisoners. Only 1,500 had been killed in action against the allies, the balance having died of disease, of starvation, or else had been killed by Portuguese irregulars.[1]

The British army had now chased the French out of Portugal for a third time, on all occasions as a result of Wellington's endeavours. Sufficiently confident that the French would be engaged in licking their wounds, the Commander-in-Chief felt able to pay a visit to Beresford on the Elvas-Badajoz front to the south. But he was aware of the resilience of the French and was not away too long.

Bevan in the meantime had to spend some days in what he described as the 'miserable' village of Nave de Aver, less than two miles from the Spanish frontier. He wrote from here in early April in cheerless weather for it was cold and raining. He was contemplating, he told Mary, the possibility of a 'second Spanish campaign', but then no one knew what exactly was in Wellington's mind. Interested in public opinion, Bevan was anxious to know 'what people think of this campaign at home. We have now been upwards of one month constantly marching with very little respite.' As usual, and an understandable preoccupation of his with so many mouths to see fed, he commented that there was not too much to eat. A loaf of white bread, a rarity, sold for nine shillings, yet 'the soldier gives the only two or three dollars he has in the world for this treat'. Two of his men out foraging in what we would call no man's land had been captured. One of them, 'provokingly' enough Bevan said, was one of their best musicians. Not forgetting that Mary appreciated military news, he told her that the troops chiefly employed in the fighting had been those from the Light Division, that is the 52nd, 43rd (Monmouths), 95th and a Portuguese regiment of riflemen (*Cacadores*) supported by Picton's 3rd Division. As for the 5th Division they had had 'plenty of fatigues but no fighting'.[2] In this letter Bevan referred to Sir Hew Dalrymple whose daughter, Arabella, Mary's brother James Dacres had married. For some reason Bevan had been against the marriage. It will be remembered that Charles had had his knife into Dalrymple over the signing of the Convention of Cintra.

Ten days later he wrote, this time in more comfort from Aldea de Obispo, a village just in Spain on the main road from Almeida to Ciudad Rodrigo:

We have at length I believe finished our chase and have the great good fortune to cast anchor in a Spanish district of a Portuguese village, inasmuch that we have a roof over our heads and chairs and table; to people who have been nearly six weeks living almost in the open air this little comfort is, I assure you, felt very much . . . We have been for the last two or three days very much harassed in blocking Almeida which is about 5 miles from hence . . . our men stand much in need of repose for we are 150 short since we left Torres Vedras. The French have left a garrison also in Ciudad Rodrigo, I believe about 5 thousand men, in Almeida about 1500. Both these places are strong.

Lord Wellington is this morning going into the Alentejo [Portuguese province to the south] we hear to superintend at the siege of Badajoz. Therefore we may expect not to move till he returns. The French Army gave out that they are going to Russia and in two years they will return and drive the English into the sea. In the meantime they have lost many men and have been very roughly handled wherever they came in contact with our troops. I am exceedingly glad to hear James has a frigate and so good a station. I hope his wife is quite well and has presented her husband with a son before his departure from home. I have not a word more about my mother's plan of living in the country. Is it given up? . . .

I have plenty to do, I assure you, our people have hardly any shoes and I am very certain I do not know where to get them nearer than Lisbon. . . . I have not heard lately from Paterson, I imagine like myself he has but little time for writing letters. He has the advantage of being in a plentiful country while we are wanting of everything. However that to me at least is no novelty, therefore I am patience itself. The weather is now very hot. 5 days ago it was the most excessively cold . . . with a continual fall of snow during the whole day. I am very tired of this campaign. We are, to use a favourite expression of yours poked away in a very bad brigade. The sooner we are out of it the better for all parties. We have only 500 men here the rest sick. I hope my little ones are all well and all very good and do not give their mother too much trouble to keep them in order. I expect to find little Charles able to read like a man. . . . Tom I expect to find extremely impudent. Edward rather [illegible] and the young lady exceedingly pert. What do you think of my ideas?[3]

A good piece of family news emerging from this letter, and one which gave Bevan pleasure, was about Mary's brother. At last James Dacres had got command of a ship, the *Guerrière*. Although this was an old worn-out frigate carrying 48 guns (and a broadside of 517 lbs) captured some years before from the French, the ship and her captain would become famous in the following year.

During the war between Britain and the United States beginning in 1812 the *Guerrière*, on her way to Halifax in Nova Scotia, fell in with the United States ship *Constitution* of 56 guns (with a broadside of 768 lbs). For an hour and three-quarters the two ships were locked in what proved to be an unequal struggle, until the *Guerrière* had lost all her masts and seventy-eight of her men killed or wounded. James Dacres received a musket ball in his back while urging on his crew, but would not leave the deck. At his court-martial for surrendering his ship he was unanimously and honourably acquitted, and with his career happily re-established he went on in 1838 to become a Rear-Admiral and eight years later was appointed Commander-in-Chief at the Cape of Good Hope.[4]

Writing on 22 April from the same place Bevan showed his continuing interest in all the doings of his old regiment, the 28th:

I was, my dearest Mary, rather premature when I told you that we were now in peaceable quarters, for the very night after I had written to you, about half past twelve, we were ordered to march to support the Light Division which were supposed to have been engaged; the enemy, however, did not choose to fight. Therefore, after having been about 14 hours under arms and marching nearly twenty miles, we returned home. We are still obliged to be very alert as the French have a strong force on the other bank of the river and as the weather is just now very bad it is not very agreeable. It is as cold and as uncomfortable here now as in the month of November in England; but we have no fireplaces nor carpets but what are made of stone. This, however, I imagine cannot last very long, and we shall soon enjoy the more enlivening beams of the sun who's cheery countenance we now seldom see.

What a noble fight the troops under General Graham have made [at the Battle of Barossa on 5 March]! I see my old Friends the 28th came in for their share. How fortunate is Col Belson. Browne of course will get a Lt Colonelcy now. I think the General is not sparing of his recommendations. I suppose the retreat of Massena and the fatigues and services of this army will not be thought of in the rejoicing over this dish of blood; so much for military fortune.

I am, and I hope you will most particularly tell her so, very much obliged to Eleanor for the Gazette: had she not sent the supplement as she did I should have thought her guilty of high treason at least. I am also very glad to hear that you are going to town for a little while. You will have the opportunity of paying your respects to Mrs Shaw and to all our friends in that part of the world, in which part I most sincerely wish I also was and that I had money enough to be comfortable in it. . . . I have had a letter from Caroline [his sister] whence I learn that nothing is decided about a place of abode.[5]

Keeping Mary posted about the movements of the generals, as he rather liked to do, he told her that Sir Brent Spencer was in command in the absence of Wellington, and that 'Sir William Erskine joins this division tomorrow'. This was because Craufurd had returned from leave to take over the Light Division and General Leith, commanding the 5th Division, was still away sick. Clearly Erskine's recent failures had not deterred Wellington from putting him in command of this Division. It is perhaps curious that Bevan did not allow himself some comment on Erskine's competency, for the army must have been only too aware of his lamentable performances in the fog.

In the second half of April, in the uplands on the frontier, there was a brief lull in the fighting. Had Bevan the time or inclination he might, being both serious-minded and reflective, have indulged in some critical self-examination. Just how would he have perceived his life's progress thus far? First he would have counted his domestic blessings. He was happily married and had a thriving young family to whom he was devoted. Marital bliss was, of course, spoilt by the constant demands made by the army for service abroad against France. There indeed was the rub. He was frustrated by the separations and by the need to earn a living by soldiering. There are signs that he now longed to sheathe his sword and lead a bucolic life with his family.

But what then of his military career, now spanning some 16 years? He may well have had some satisfaction at having reached the giddy heights of lieutenant-colonel, while having at the same time reservations on whether the purchase money laid out had been well spent. As for his experience in the field he might have been disappointed with the amount of action he had so far seen. He could point to the Egyptian campaign of 1801 and to serving with Moore in 1808/9. On the other hand the expeditions to north Germany, Copenhagen, Sweden and the Scheldt had produced, for him, no fighting. In the present campaign, so far lasting only some weeks, there had been the constant promise of action – but as yet no more – which might prove his capabilities as a regimental commander in the field.

On a different tack, how would a superior assess his professional talents? First he had amply demonstrated in Egypt and during the retreat to Corunna that he possessed the physical courage needed for a soldier in that day and age. Then he had shown efficiency both as a regimental soldier and as Paget's principal staff officer. His acute intelligence would always be an asset and he seemed, also, to be interested in the broad picture of a campaign, not just in what was happening in his own backyard. But as to how good a commanding officer he was proving to be we are short of information. The signs are that, even if he had so far been insufficiently tested in the field, he was conscientious about his men's welfare and that he took his responsibilities seriously.

Lastly there was his temperament. How suited was he to the military life and what of his staying power? His impatience notwithstanding, he appeared to accept with fairly good grace the hardships of campaigning. But his tendency towards suffering from bouts of depression and a proneness to self-pity are more troublesome traits. Could these have impeded him from carrying out his duties properly? All we can say is that there is no evidence that this was so, or that he lacked powers of endurance.

Since January a change had come about in Bevan's life. Now at last in the heart of the Iberian landmass there was a clear objective before him. His purpose was to serve his country in the field and defeat the French. The dark thoughts that had sometimes dogged him at Ceuta and elsewhere seem to have been banished. At least there was no sign of them in his correspondence with Mary. As we consider Bevan standing on the threshold of great events at the beginning of May 1811, the prospects for him looked good.

*   *   *   *

As if anxious to redeem himself and his military reputation, Masséna was ready in less than three weeks after his defeat at Sabugal to launch a counter-attack against Wellington from the position occupied by his troops behind the Azaba River a few miles west of Ciudad Rodrigo. One of Masséna's reasons for embarking on this initiative was his determination to relieve the garrison at Almeida. During the Peninsular Wars Almeida was one of four fortresses situated in pairs on the frontier between Spain and Portugal. These pairs, Almeida/Ciudad Rodrigo and Elvas/Badajoz, held, as perceived by the military commanders, the keys to the door for those leading armies west into Portugal or east into Spain. Thus it was essential for Wellington, if he was to take the road to Salamanca and Burgos, to hold the former pair, just as the French needed to command the same pair should they remount an attack on Portugal.

By now Masséna had received reinforcements from Marshal Bessières and his Army of the North, notably of cavalry, and so had a numerical superiority over the allied army, with some 46,500 men, including 4,500 cavalry, under him, compared to Wellington's 37,500. But if the allies had less cavalry then they had more guns: 48 guns to the French 38.[6] Some of the troops under his command were not available to Wellington to counter a French attack. These were Pack's Portuguese brigade, the 2nd

134

Foot (the Queen's) and some cavalry units who were all engaged in blockading the French garrison at Almeida.

Wellington, back on 28 April at his headquarters at Vila Formoso after his visit to the southern sector, realized – he was well served by his spies – that an attack by Masséna was pending. He therefore chose a defensive position for his forces extending more than 10 miles along the top of a ridge between the Turon and Dos Casas streams. At its centre was the village of Fuentes de Oñoro which sloped down to the latter of the two rivers. His northern flank rested near the ruined Fort Conception, almost adjacent to Aldea de Obispo, and the southern one went nearly as far as Nave de Aver. As might have been expected, Picton's 3rd Division and Craufurd's Light Division were in the centre of the line, while specially picked Light companies were placed in the village of Fuentes de Oñoro. The newly raised, and therefore in-experienced, 7th Division was on the right. On the left, facing Reynier's corps of 10,000 and separated from the French by the Dos Casas, there running through a deep ravine, were the 5th Division, now under Erskine, and the 6th, under Alexander Campbell.

Historians regard the Battle at Fuentes de Oñoro as an important one in the roll call of Wellington's campaigns and Oman devotes no less than 39 pages to it in his great history of the war, stating it has been called the most hazardous of all Wellington's fights. Wellington himself did not regard the battle as a victory – nor though as a defeat – and wrote that the Secretary of State 'was quite right not to move [a vote] of thanks [in Parliament] for the battle, though it was the most difficult I was ever concerned in. If Boney had been there we should have been beat'.[7] Wellington had even admitted he was at fault before the battle in extending his line too far to the south. This sort of admission was extremely rare for Wellington who normally always thought he was right.

There have been many descriptions of this battle and we do not need to give the reader a blow by blow account of it, especially as

Bevan and his Regiment were denied any moment of glory during its course. Suffice it to summarize the salient events which took place and which break down into two separate parts.

On 3 May Masséna made a head-on attack with fourteen battalions on the British position in the village of Fuentes de Oñoro. The fighting was heavy and at one time the French battled their way up through the village, only to be thrown back onto the eastern bank of the Dos Casas by the end of the day. On 4 May there was no fighting, only exchanges of fire and French reconnaissances seeking to find any weak points in the allied line.

The main French attack came the next day on 5 May. First their cavalry, moving in great strength against Wellington's right flank, succeeded in occupying Nave de Aver and then in successfully attacking the 7th Division, which fell back under the weight of the onslaught. To cover their retreat and plug an opening gap, Wellington despatched the indomitable Light Division, who, forming unassailable squares, were able to stabilize the position. Wellington then decided to swing his whole line through 90 degrees with Fuentes de Oñoro acting as a pivot, to face what appeared to be the gathering of a strong French deployment on his new southern flank. In fact a French attack here never materialized and the enemy, it is usually agreed, missed his chance. The superior British artillery played an important role at this juncture. Meanwhile Masséna had renewed his previous attack on Fuentes de Oñoro, which consequently saw the bitterest fighting of the day. The French were not far from achieving their object of reaching the upper part of the village when at a critical moment the 88th Regiment (Connaught Rangers) led a gallant counterattack which helped to retrieve the situation. Eventually, once again as on 3 May, the French were driven back to their start line. Their attacks were not renewed and the battle was effectively over.

On the allied left the 5th Division merely had to contend, both days, with 'demonstrations' by Reynier, which involved some local skirmishing. On 3 May there were no casualties at all in the Division, and two days later only twenty-one men were wounded.

Overall allied losses for the two days fighting were 1,804 (killed, wounded and missing) as compared to the enemy's 2,844.[8] Bevan described to Mary in a letter written just four days after the battle from the 'heights near Alameida' (he meant Alameda, not to be confused with Almeida), what happened:

We have, my dearest Mary, now been seven days perched upon the hills opposite the French Army under Masséna hourly expecting to engage; on the 5th there took place a very [illegible] affair on the right; the Enemy was repulsed in his attempt to turn on our right flank with considerable loss, that on our side was also severe, but I do not really know what; report says from 12 to 1300 killed and wounded. The attack on the part of the Enemy was chiefly made by cavalry, all beastly drunk. Our Division is on the left when they only skirmished and wounded about 35 or 40 men. The Light Companies only were engaged, that of the 4th fortunately did not lose a man. We are now quite at a loss to guess what the Enemy is about. It was yesterday reported that they were on the retreat but whether to make their attack on another part of the front or to fall back has not yet been properly ascertainable. However, do what we can they must be beaten. This Army is in high spirits and confident of success.[9]

As Commanding Officer of his Regiment it must have been a disappointment to Bevan that, yet again, his men had been denied a part in the battle, and that he himself had been unable to show his paces as a commander in the field. He must have felt his earlier negative assessment of the brigade the 4th was in under Dunlop was the correct one. At the same time Wellington seemed disinclined, for whatever reason, to entrust the 5th Division with any kind of lead role.

CHAPTER TWELVE

Almeida: The Garrison Escapes

The day after the battle of Fuentes de Oñoro all was quiet on the front line between the two opposing armies. The allied and French forces continued to face each other with the River Dos Casas between them, but neither side took any offensive action. The British improved their defences, while both armies attended to their wounded and buried their dead.

It was the same on 7 May, another day of inactivity for the soldiers. But by now Masséna had decided that he would not be able to relieve Almeida. Instead he would have to retreat and then regroup in Spain. Consequently he ordered the huge supply of food brought up in a convoy for the beleaguered garrison, and which had remained at Gallegos during the fighting, to be distributed among his troops.[1] If he could not rescue the garrison he did not want Brenier's 1,400 men to fall into allied hands as prisoners, so he determined that they should break out from Almeida, having rendered the fortifications useless, and rejoin the Army of Portugal in Spain. As he was unable to communicate with Brenier he called for volunteers to try and get through the allied lines and deliver to the governor a message in cipher with his instructions. He offered a reward of 6,000 francs to any man who could accomplish this dangerous mission. Three men came forward. One Corporal Pierre Zaniboni, disguised himself as a Spanish trader selling tobacco and buying the clothes of men who had been killed. Another, Jean-Nöel Lami, was dressed as a Portuguese peasant and also pretended to be a pedlar. The two men were caught and their

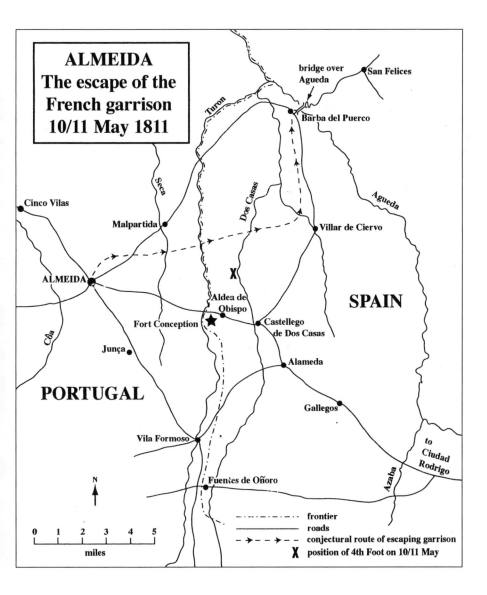

ALMEIDA
The escape of the French garrison 10/11 May 1811

bridge over Agueda

San Felices

Turon

Barba del Puerco

Seca

Cinco Vilas

Dos Casas

Agueda

Malpartida

Villar de Ciervo

ALMEIDA

X

SPAIN

Aldea de Obispo

Fort Conception

Castellego de Dos Casas

Côa

Junça

Alameda

PORTUGAL

Gallegos

to Ciudad Rodrigo

Vila Formoso

N

Azaba

Fuentes de Oñoro

frontier
roads
conjectural route of escaping garrison
X position of 4th Foot on 10/11 May

0 1 2 3 4 5
miles

letters of instruction discovered on their persons. So, in accordance with the laws of war, they were shot as spies. The third, a light infantryman called André Tillet, preferred to wear uniform. He crawled in the dark for some way down the ravine through which the Dos Casas flowed. At length he emerged and then proceeded westward creeping on all fours through fields of corn. Successfully avoiding the allied pickets encircling Almeida, he pluckily reached his destination, where before dawn on 7 May he delivered his instructions to Brenier. For his exploit Tillet was promoted sergeant and awarded the Legion of Honour. He was also granted a handsome pension.[2] That night Brenier, as instructed by Masséna, fired salvos of his big guns to show he had received his orders to evacuate his garrison and rejoin the French army. These orders recommended that he try a northerly line and make for the bridge at Barba del Puerco.

The way was now clear for Masséna to begin his withdrawal. The 6th and 9th Corps began retiring on 8 May, while the 2nd Corps under Reynier moved north to San Felices well to the north-west of Ciudad Rodrigo and three or four miles to the east of the village of Barba del Puerco. As a result of these movements Wellington pushed forward his outposts and resumed his blockading of Almeida, Major-General Alexander Campbell and his 6th Division taking over from Pack. Campbell, allowed by Wellington discretion as to where he posted his blockading force, then disposed of the brigades under his command as follows: Baron Eben and his Portuguese brigade was in the vicinity of Junça about three and a half miles away from Almeida on the south side; Hulse's brigade of three battalions was in the west some distance from the town; Pack's independent Portuguese brigade were at Cinco Vilas four or five miles away from Almeida to the north, while finally Burne's brigade was stationed to the east of the fortress town. The 2nd Foot (the Queen's) under Lieutenant-Colonel Iremonger, part of Burne's troops, were positioned next to the most southerly of Pack's units about a mile from the town and nearest of all Campbell's division to Almeida. In addition Barbacena's cavalry brigade, which had a roving commission in the area of the lower Agueda, came under Campbell's command. Campbell himself, as well as Burne, was at Malpartida. The former evidently thought the arrangements he had made were satisfactory. These included a system of pickets which he had inherited from Pack whereby the officer in command of each detachment of troops on picket duty had delegated authority to act as he thought fit in the face of the enemy. Nevertheless, Campbell was later criticized for having placed his troops too far away from Almeida and for neglecting to see that the pickets were pushed up to the walls of the town at night. Also it was argued that the garrison was unlikely to attempt an escape on the southern or western side of the town but was far more likely to make the attempt on the eastern side and aim for the bridge over the Agueda close to Barba del Puerco, even if this was over 10 miles away from Almeida as the crow flies.[3] Campbell's dispositions should have reflected, so the argument ran, what was most likely to happen when Brenier broke out, that is the cordon should have been stronger to the east of Almeida. The critics, with their advantage of hindsight, were doubtless right on all counts.

But the defensive measures to prevent the escape of the garrison, which were to affect Bevan so profoundly, have not yet been fully described. At 6 pm on 9 May Colonel George Murray, Wellington's able Quartermaster General at army headquarters at Vila Formoso – his post was about as close as you could get in those days to our own Chief of Staff today – had directed General Erskine, still in command of the 5th, as follows:

Lord Wellington desires that you will be so good as push one Battalion of infantry to your left to the distance of two or three miles beyond Fort Conception. This battalion should place pickets at the passes over the Dos Casas riverlet which lead from the side of Villar de Ciervo and Barba del Puerco

141

towards Malpartida, and should communicate to the rear with Br-Gen Pack at Malpartida. It had better be moved to its station at dusk and should take care to conceal its post and its force as much as possible from the enemy. Your communication with that Battalion can easily be kept up by the cavalry and you will be so good as have a connection established from its left by means of the Portuguese Dragoons under your orders with the other Regt. of Colonel Barbacena's cavalry which is upon the lower Agueda and reports to Br. Gen Pack to whom I beg you will be so good as communicate your arrangements above alluded to.[4]

The 5th Division, we should explain, was located in the Aldea de Obispo-Castellego de Dos Casas – Alameda area.

Finally a further order, a written one, was sent in the early afternoon of 10 May by Wellington, who had been on reconnaissance that morning, to Erskine, ordering him, in the words used by Wellington in his official despatch to Liverpool 'to send a battalion to Barba del Puerco to guard the bridge there, which had been previously ordered, and had been posted, to observe the passages of the Dos Casas between Aldea de Obispo and Barba del Puerco'.[5]

Clearly Wellington had concluded on the morning of 10 May that the all-important bridge over the Agueda at Barba del Puerco must at all costs be defended to thwart any attempt by the Almeida garrison to use it as an escape route back to rejoin the Army of Portugal. In fact his order of 9 May, as he must have come to realize, had not extended his line sufficiently north to cover this contingency. While Campbell called on Wellington between 5.30 and 6.00 pm in the late afternoon of 10 May to report that all his dispositions round Almeida would be in place before dark, Erskine made no similiar report about the bridge being guarded.

We need now to say something more about this bridge and its surroundings. First its dramatic setting. The Roman bridge lay some three miles into Spain and just over 1000 yards east of the village of Barba del Puerco at the bottom of a narrow winding gorge hundreds of feet deep. Constructed with three stone arches with a total length of 350 feet and a width of 15 feet, it spanned the River Agueda whose bed was composed of masses of broken rock and which, in full spring spate, could contain a rushing torrent. From each side the bridge was approached by a steep and narrow zig-zag track. Above it the village of Barba del Puerco was served on its western side by a road coming up from Malpartida in Portugal and from the southern by a road from Villar de Ciervo in Spain. Beyond the bridge to the east the track was the road to San Felices. For some miles before reaching the village the road from Villar de Ciervo followed the course of a long ridge over 2000 feet high giving views to the west and east. On account of the topography to deny access to the bridge to an enemy wishing to cross it going from the west to the east, as Brenier might be expected to go, defensive troops would essentially need to position themselves on the high ground above the gorge and just to the east of the village of Barba del Puerco.

In differing circumstances this bridge had briefly been the scene in March 1810 of an ugly skirmish between the British and French. This had happened when the French were probing from the east and towards Portugal. Several companies of the 95th Regiment were occupying Barba del Puerco with one of them, comprising 200 men, posted below in the gorge at the bridge. Six hundred French from San Felices to the east had on a dirty night tried to surprise the outpost on the bridge. It was a desperate encounter and the French were only beaten off after reinforcements from the 95th came down from the village above.[6]

The battalion chosen on 9 May to occupy the advanced post 'two or three miles beyond Ford Conception' was Bevan's 4th Foot. The location where Bevan and his Regiment found themselves the next day was, as Bevan himself later related, by a bridge on the Dos Casas River. As the crow flies they would have been seven or eight miles from the village of Barba del Puerco. Over the broken and wooded country between their location and the village the distance on the march would probably have been a mile or two further.

These distances are important, as will be seen as the story unfolds.

The fact that the 4th had been selected for this role would have come as no surprise to the troops of the 5th Division, for the Regiment had had a long and distinguished record in the wars against Napoleon. The other two regiments in Dunlop's brigade, the 30th and 44th, were far less experienced, and Bevan seemed to have a poor opinion of them.

The rest of the army resumed their stations well to the south-east of Almeida and between the Côa and Azaba Rivers. Wellington must have considered that he had given all the necessary instructions to prevent the escape of the Almeida garrison by the blockading troops. His foe, then, would have been in a trap, or so he thought, and if an attempt to break out were made, as to Wellington and Campbell seemed likely, then the garrison would fall victim to the encircling troops. Alternatively, if the French stayed put they would be forced to surrender when their food supplies ran out. Either way a good haul of prisoners, including General Brenier, could be expected.

There was one particular reason, not known to the army at the time, why Wellington wished to see Brenier taken prisoner. Two years earlier Brenier had been captured at the Battle of Vimeiro and then transferred to London, where, on parole, he proceeded to get into debt. Rather impertinently he had asked Sir Arthur Wellesley, as he then was, for a loan of £500.[7] The loan was made and Brenier was then repatriated to France, but up to the time of the siege of Almeida no repayment of the loan had been made. No wonder Wellington looked forward to having the Frenchman as his captive. There would presumably be no second parole this time!

In the meantime Brenier himself had, during 8 and 9 May, been preparing the necessary demolition charges in Almeida in order to render the fortress and its guns useless to the allies. He mined the fortifications (140 mines were used) and spiked his guns. One ingenious method he used to do this was to place the muzzle of one gun against and at right angles to another and then firing both guns simultaneously so that the shot of one going off in the direction of the besiegers muffled the shot of the other.[8] The result of this subterfuge was that Campbell's men were unaware that Brenier was destroying his guns, and consequently that an evacuation of the garrison was imminent. The French ruse thus lulled the besiegers into a false sense of security.

At last Brenier's operations were completed and he was ready to leave the fortress town. Earlier he had called together his senior officers, read them his orders from Masséna and briefed them on the hazards of the forthcoming operation. Their objective, he explained, was to reach the bridge over the Agueda River close to Barba del Puerco and then rejoin their compatriots in the Army of Portugal at San Felices (the distance from Almeida to the bridge, we calculate, was some 13 miles by the route that was in the event taken by the French). Brenier had also walked round the town and along the ramparts talking to his soldiers and reassuring them about what lay ahead. He found them, he reported, confident and enthusiastic.[9]

So on the night of 10 May in bright moonlight two silent French columns numbering some 1,400 men began leaving Almeida at about 11.30 pm by, according to Oman, the north gate. They were led by two elite companies of the 50th battalion of the 82nd Regiment. As Brenier, in the rear, left the town he gave orders to battalion commander Morlet to light the demolition fuses. When this was done and the sappers were sure that the inhabitants of the town were not going to interrupt the operation, the demolition teams hastened to join the escaping, and still unobserved, columns and act as their rearguard. Brenier had both guile and a ruthless streak in him. He reported that he had 'arranged that the baggage train would be at the rear of the columns. I foresaw that very probably they would not be able to keep up with us.'[10] This did not bother the French commander as he thought the allies' attention would be diverted by capturing the baggage and its minders.

As soon as the columns had cleared the gate they turned to the east and, avoiding roads, set off in close formation for their distant objective, knowing that they would have shortly to pierce the allied cordon and pickets lying in their way. For a first-hand account of Brenier's march we may rely on Brenier's quite detailed report written on 17 May at Salamanca and addressed to Marshal Marmont,[11] the newly appointed French commander of the Army of Portugal. Unhappily for the French, this report was intercepted by the allies and eventually fell into Wellington's hands. Brenier, in writing his report, considered his plans had been 'perfectly carried out'. Thus the leading elements of his columns reached the actual outposts in the cordon at the exact time the explosives in Almeida went off – around midnight according to most commentators. His force broke through the pickets and, in his words:

> I quickly advanced along my route, continuously harassed on my flanks and at my rear, as I had thought would happen. All the baggage trains were pillaged. I had not wanted a guide because he would only have been able to give me information about paths that I had no wish to follow and also because he might have made us uncertain about the route we were planning to take. Not being able to reconnoitre by night the different routes that I had studied for a long time by day, the moon was my compass. The various streams and rivers that I crossed, whose locations I was already aware of, helped me find my route. I was harassed as far as Turon, where they then left me. Finally, at dawn, I found myself between Villar de Ciervo and Barba de Puerco. I then aimed for the Agueda. Between these two villages, and before I had reached the crest of the ridge, the enemy cavalry appeared on my right and marched parallel with me, firing on me, in order either to stop me or to indicate to the troops following me the route I had taken. To my left I could see a number of ridges crowned with troops, I took steps to avoid them. I finally arrived at a path which led to the bridge of San Felices [that is of Barba del Puerco].

The two columns that all the time marched within sight of each other and within range of each other, arrived together at the left bank of the Agueda in the same order as they had set out from Almeida. They had marched the whole way section by section, despite the rocks, rivers and gorges.

The rearguard of sappers had just joined the rear of the left-hand column. I then saw that there were some troops on the other side [of the river]. By using a telescope, I could see that they were French so we quickly climbed down to the bridge. The enemy was arriving from all sides and had reached the rear of our column. Then it was with sorrow that I saw some of our brave comrades perish. Finally, General Reynier, commanding the 2nd Corps, sent troops down towards the bridge and covered our passage. He gathered all the wounded and had them taken to San Felices, where we were reunited with about 1,000 men. In the whole of this operation I lost 360 men, of which about 150 were killed, mostly in the gorge, and 200 hundred prisoners, who became separated, not being able to keep up with the rapid march of the column.[12]

Brenier had obviously thought out the route he should take with considerable care. First he needed to steer well clear of Malpartida, Campbell's headquarters; this therefore precluded his using the rather roundabout Malpartida to Barba del Puerco road. Then he probably concluded that it would be more prudent in any case to approach the bridge from the south rather than from the west or south-west, when he would have needed to have overcome the obstacles presented by the lower Dos Casas, which, like the Agueda, ran through some deep gorges, and eventually by the actual village of Barba del Puerco. He therefore marched first in an easterly direction, deliberately aiming to join, in due course, the Villar de Ciervo to Barba del Puerco road which ran north along a ridge to his destination. This planned route – he was not to know it – took him quite close to where Bevan and the 4th Foot had been posted north of Fort Conception. One thing, almost

147

above all others that night, Brenier must have been extremely thankful for. The bridge at Barba del Puerco he found, on reaching it, to be unguarded by the allies.

For the action taken by the allies to frustrate Brenier's march that night we have to rely essentially on reports written by Campbell and Pack.[13] In making his report to Campbell, Pack said he could give no satisfactory explanation as to why the allied pickets did not 'close' on the enemy and did not, as instructed, 'try to retard' progress by the French; admittedly one outpost had offered for a moment some resistance and had taken casualties in doing so. The two allied commanding officers whose units were in the area where the cordon was pierced were both singularly ineffectual, not that this was stated by Pack or Campbell. Colonel do Rogo of the 4th Portuguese Cacadores took not the slightest bit of notice of what had happened to his sentries. Just to his south Lieutenant-Colonel Iremonger of the 2nd Foot was similarly passive but he at least sent out some patrols, though not in the direction of Malpartida. These came back eventually to report that the fortress had been evacuated and that the French had gone off to the north somewhere. Iremonger made, it seemed, no further effort to locate the enemy. Even at dawn his regiment had not moved from its original position. Later he was to dispute that Brenier could have passed close to him.

Not everyone, fortunately, was so supine as do Rogo and Iremonger. Pack himself, roused by the commotion at the picket line, hastily collected together eighty men of the 1st Portuguese and set off in pursuit of the foe, though not before he had sent messages that he was following the French to Campbell at Malpartida and to Major Dursbach of the 1st Portuguese who was positioned behind the cordon. Hurrying for all he was worth, Pack caught up the rear of the retreating columns and then for several hours kept up a running fire on them, taking stragglers prisoner and capturing the French baggage. Brenier's march, Pack stated with obvious admiration, was 'rapid and compact' and was made in perfect silence, not a shot being fired by his men before daybreak. Further, the French general found his way 'through a very intricate country by paths but little frequented'. Eventually Pack found himself reduced to a major, a sergeant and just ten men, though still on the heels of the French. It was now that he was joined by an English cavalryman, a Captain Beresford, who was instrumental in rousing a troop of fifty dragoons stationed at Villar de Ciervo. They were from the 1st Royals of Slade's brigade and had been tasked with watching the Agueda to their east. The dragoons skirmished with the French and caused them to delay.[14]

Another officer who showed initiative that night was Lieutenant-Colonel Douglas, commanding the 8th Portuguese Regiment at Junça, south-east of Almeida. Douglas had set off quite independently for Barba del Puerco after being alerted by the explosions in Almeida. With a fine sense of urgency and thanks to good guides, he succeeded in reaching the bridge before daybreak. But neither there, nor in the vicinity, did he find any signs of the fugitive garrison. So, as everything seemed quiet, Douglas turned away to search for the enemy elsewhere.[15] It need hardly be said that, if the 8th Portuguese had stayed their hand a little longer, Brenier would have run right into them.

Meanwhile Campbell, on receiving Pack's message at Malpartida, at once called out the 36th Foot (the Herefordshires) under the fiery Colonel Basil Cochrane and sent men off in all directions to locate the enemy or the route they had taken. Some grenadiers were detached to the right, while eight companies of the 36th eventually got onto Brenier's tracks, a peasant having given information that the French had been seen heading towards Villar de Ciervo. At last Campbell's force managed to catch up with the rear of Brenier's columns, just as the leading French were nearing the bridge at Barba del Puerco. Campbell, as he reported to Wellington, was

> most opportunely joined by Lieut.Col. Bevan with 9 companies of the 4th regt., and soon after by Lieut.Col. Visconde de Barbacena with a squadron of dragoons, from

149

whom, as well as from Lieut.Col. Bevan, I received the greatest assistance and support.[16]

Now – and the time was around 6 am – there came to be enacted a scene of the utmost confusion. Seeing that Brenier's men were about to gain their objective Campbell ordered the 36th to throw off their packs and run towards the French in a last desperate effort to head them away from the gorge and bridge. The British were too late to prevent the first column from reaching and then crossing the bridge, but the second one was caught as it began its difficult descent to the river by the steep narrow track. By now the British were above their foe and began to pour down on the heads of the Frenchmen a deadly fire from their muskets. In trying to hurry and avoid this fire many of the enemy soldiers lost their footing and plunged down the precipitous slopes. Some were shot, some had broken necks and limbs and some were drowned in the river below. But, despite Campbell's far too optimistic report to Wellington on the casualties inflicted, a large majority of the French gained the safety of the eastern side of the Agueda. They were given notable help by a sizeable detachment of troops sent by Reynier from his 2nd Corps stationed at nearby San Felices. For when Reynier heard distant firing, as Brenier was making his way towards Barba del Puerco, he reacted quickly sending his men to give the escaping garrison much-needed covering fire from his side of the river.[17]

There was a violent postscript to Campbell's efforts to stop the French. Colonel Cochrane of the 36th, in what was described as a 'rash enterprise', tried, as he saw it, to retrieve the situation. Without orders from Campbell, he spontaneously led a mixed force of his Regiment together with some men from the 4th across the bridge and up the steep track on the opposite side. This storming party, heavily outnumbered by Reynier's men, were beaten back and suffered considerable casualties, losing eighteen killed and wounded, and seventeen men, including an officer, taken prisoner. Of these the 4th lost two killed and eleven wounded, including a lieutenant.[18]

In this way ended a less than glorious episode in the annals of the British army. Yet the escape of the French garrison from Almeida was a worthy feat of arms, even if Brenier's troops had suffered quite heavy casualties. For his achievement in bringing 1000 men through many miles of territory controlled by the allies to rejoin the Army of Portugal, Napoleon immediately promoted Brenier to General of Division.

As for the allies, Wellington was furious at the failure of his forces to stop Brenier's escape, calling it 'the most disgraceful military event which has yet occurred in the peninsular wars'.[19] For him one particular failure was to stand out before all others. He had specifically ordered the bridge at Barba del Puerco to be guarded, and his order had not been carried out. The task had been given to Bevan's Regiment. Why were the 4th Foot not in place? Something had gone badly wrong, and we will examine what had happened in the next chapter.

CHAPTER THIRTEEN

Almeida and the
4th Regiment of Foot

It looked as if, on the night of 10/11 May, Charles Bevan had been given a fine opportunity to show his mettle as a soldier and commanding officer. In fact the task of denying Brenier and his men the use of the bridge at Barba del Puerco was just the kind of operation which we might expect Bevan to have relished. After all there was something of the heroic about his allotted role, even if it could not quite be compared to how Horatius famously held the bridge across the Tiber in 505 B.C. against the army of the Etruscans on their march on Rome. Yet, although the 4th were ordered to the bridge, they never reached their destination in time and 1000 Frenchmen were able to pass over it into safety and out of Wellington's clutches. Of course there were a number of reasons for the British calamity, and we have already touched on some of the criticisms levelled at General Campbell. The 4th's failure to be in the right place at the right time was just one of several reasons for Brenier's triumph, even if it was an important one

As we saw in the last chapter there are, discounting Wellington's despatches, a number of useful accounts of the escape of the French garrison to draw on, notably those of Brenier, Pack and Campbell, but none of these tell us about the exact movements of the 4th Foot on the night of 10/11 May. From the pen of Charles

Bevan, however, we do have two brief accounts of what his Regiment was up to that night. First, in a laconic reference to the affair at Barba del Puerco, he told Mary:

> We had a skirmish with the garrison of Almeida on their retreat but were unfortunately a little too late to do more than what you will see by the Papers took place – their escape is a matter of great annoyance to us all.[1]

Second, there was a short letter he wrote on 11 May from Barba del Puerco to, we must presume, Brigadier Dunlop, for onward transmission to Erskine, explaining why he was not at the bridge at an earlier time. He said:

> I beg leave to inform you, for the information of Major-General Sir William Erskine, that I arrived here [Barba del Puerco] with the 4th Regiment about 6 this morning. And further, as a reason for my not having marched last night, that, although I had ascertained that one party of the enemy's troops had crossed the river, I was by no means certain that others were not moving in the same direction. I therefore thought it might be more essential to retain my position at the bridge and march in the morning, which I accordingly did, having sent a patrol from the Portuguese to reconnoitre Barba de[l] Puerco.[2]

This letter is for us highly important and presently we shall consider it in some detail.

In the meantime we will look critically at the chain of events which led from the issuing of Wellington's order to Erskine on 10 May to the late arrival of Bevan and his Regiment at the bridge over the Agueda at Barba del Puerco early on the morning of 11 May. We will take these events in strict chronological order.

The Issuing of Wellington's order of 10 May to Erskine

It is well known that Wellington took great pains in drafting his despatches to his political masters. After all, he knew that, as often as not, they would appear as the official version of events in *The London Gazette.* Wellington's instructions to his subordinates in the field were in a somewhat different category. At the time in question Wellington's usual practice was to issue these, as we have seen, through his Quartermaster-General. With regard to the above order to which specific reference has been made on p.142, it was issued 'about 1 pm' from Wellington's headquarters at Vila Formoso, according to Wellington's unofficial letter to Lord Liverpool of 15 May. However, the precise wording of this order is not known, the text apparently not having survived. Thus we have to rely on what Wellington reported to the War Minister, that he ordered Erskine 'to send a battalion to Barba del Puerco to guard the bridge there, which had been previously ordered, and had been posted, to observe the passages of the Dos Casas between Aldea de Obispo and Barba del Puerco'.[3] Perhaps the grammar of this order is not everything it should be for purists, but the meaning becomes clear enough when it is realized that 'which' refers to 'battalion'.

While reminiscing with Lord Stanhope in 1836 about the escape of the French garrison from Almeida, Wellington was certainly wrong in so far as he averred that 'he sent orders to Colonel Bevan to march to Barba del Puerco and occupy the bridge'.[4] Of course the Commander-in-Chief would not issue such an order, unless exceptionally in the heat of battle, to a commanding officer of a regiment, nor did he, as we have seen. Certainly there is no dispute at all among the authorities that the order went to Erskine in the first instance.

The receipt of Wellington's order of 10 May by Erskine

On 10 May Erskine was dining at army headquarters at Vila Formoso with Sir Brent Spencer, commanding the 1st Division, and in the words used by Wellington to Liverpool 'received his

154

orders about 4 o'clock'.[5] This is the time that most commentators, including the historians Charles Oman, Cowper and Longford, are agreed that the order reached Erskine. One contemporary diarist, Captain Tomkinson of the 16th Light Dragoons, gave the time as 2 o'clock[6], and the historian Maxwell quotes this time too. We prefer to side with the majority view that it was 4 o'clock. Why then, it may be asked, did the order take three hours to reach Erskine, especially if he was at army headquarters where the order originated? This is a point, even if a minor one, which never seems to have been addressed. Presumably the explanation is that Erskine was expected to be located with his rather spread-out Division and, on finding he was not, the messenger had to double back some six miles to headquarters. All this would have taken some time.

Action by Erskine on receipt of Wellington's order of 10 May

Wellington in his already quoted letter to Liverpool stated:

> [Erskine] says he sent [his orders] off forthwith to the 4th Regiment which was stationed, under former orders, on the Dos Casas, halfway between Aldea de[l] Obispo and Barba del Puerco.[7]

There are two points to make here. The first concerns the exact location of the 4th on the afternoon of 10 May. By 'former orders' Wellington was referring to his order of 9 May (quoted at p.141) which instructed Erskine to post one battalion, namely the 4th Regiment, to a position 'two or three miles north of Fort Conception'. And this is where they were. The distance from Fort Conception (or Aldea de Obispo which was practically next door to the fort) to Barba del Puerco was not far short of ten miles as the crow flies. Therefore, pin-pointing the position still more critically, the 4th were seven to eight miles from Barba del Puerco. It follows that Wellington was wrong to state the 4th were 'half way' between Aldea de Obispo and Barba del Puerco. He was in error

155

by two to three miles. Second, did Erskine really send the order 'forthwith' to Bevan? Commentators, both contemporary diarists and historians, appear united on this point. He did not. To take the historians first, Oman states that Erskine held 'an important order back . . . [for] six or seven hours'. Fortescue talks of Erskine neglecting 'to transmit the orders to the 4th Regiment to proceed to Barba del Puerco until midnight'. Maxwell, writing before Oman and Fortescue, similarly says that Erkine did not send the order on 'till midnight'. Cowper, in his regimental history of the 4th, accepts that the order did not reach Bevan until 'nearly midnight'.[8]

William Napier, who was in Wellington's army at the time and who had fought at Fuentes de Oñoro, went so far as to write that Erskine 'sent no order to the fourth regiment'. Of the other contemporaries commenting on the episode, Tomkinson stated that Erskine 'put [the order] in his pocket and did not despatch the letter to Colonel Bevan before midnight'. Major George Simmons of the 95th (in the Light Division) said that Erskine 'by accident' did not send the order to Bevan in time, while an officer in the Guards wrote in his diary, published anonymously, that 'instead of promulgating them [the orders] *immediately*, the General put them in his pocket and forgot them so that the troops 'arrived too late to prevent' the garrison's escape.[9] Of course it has to be recognized in quoting these various contemporary sources that one might have been relying on another for his information.

In slightly lighter vein Edward Pakenham, the Assistant Adjutant-General at the time, and a man destined the following year to command a division at the Battle of Salamanca, was present when Erskine and Brent Spencer were dining together. His brother, Major Hercules Pakenham, then in Picton's 3rd Division, reported to his father Lord Longford that Erskine, on receipt of the order, proposed at first sending one corporal and four men to occupy the bridge. Edward remonstrated, going so far as to say, 'Sir William, you might as well attempt to block up the bridge with a pinch of this snuff (they were taking some) as to place such a party for such an object'.[10] This story, quoted by Elizabeth Longford in her biography of Wellington, shows Erskine as either a consummate joker or just plain irresponsible. No wonder Longford uses the epithet 'preposterous' to describe him.[11] It is, alas, only too easy to imagine him playing cards or drinking heavily, or both, far into the evening with the order unattended to, stuffed into his pocket. Years later Bevan's brother-in-law James Dacres said that Erskine was indeed reputed to be drunk that evening.[12] It is worth pointing out that when Erskine did finally deal with Wellington's order there is no suggestion by any of the authorities that it was sent to Bevan via the brigade commander, Dunlop. It is presumed to have gone direct to Bevan.

Action by Bevan on 10/11 May on receipt of his orders from Erskine

According to Oman, Bevan always maintained that he got nothing from Erskine until 'nearly midnight'. (Unfortunately Oman gives no hint as to where he obtained this valuable piece of information.) This certainly agrees with the other information which has just been cited. One may, therefore, conclude, in the light of the overwhelming evidence, that Bevan received his orders from Erskine very late indeed and probably not much before midnight. Once Bevan had these orders, and we must assume that Erskine's order to Bevan replicated Wellington's, that is that the battalion should march to guard the bridge at Barba del Puerco, a certain mist descends on the scene. One thing nevertheless seems clear. For some three hours or so Bevan took no steps to move his Regiment towards Barba del Puerco.

Quite apart from Wellington's own despatches, discussed in more detail later, there are now two significant items of evidence to consider. The first of these, which no historian apart from the respected Ward has considered, is the letter written by Bevan himself on 11 May to his superiors, giving his reasons for 'not having marched' earlier for the bridge at Barba del Puerco. In this explanation we have Bevan in effect admitting that he delayed. It is a nice point whether or not Bevan perceived Erskine's orders as giving him some discretion as to when he should march. If he did not, then he took a bold course indeed in deciding to delay.

Undoubtedly Bevan must have been in something of a quandary that night. Given that there were 'the enemy's troops' in the vicinity, should he, he might legitimately ask, give up his position guarding the 'bridge' over the Dos Casas? (Actually, there were a surprising number of troops moving around that night somewhere to his front. As well as Brenier's men, there were Pack's and Campbell's and several hundred of Douglas's regiment hurrying from Junça to Barba del Puerco.) If he left what he saw to be a tactically important position in order to plunge off in the darkness to reach the bridge somewhere seven or eight miles, as the crow flies, to the north, would he then be risking letting enemy units have a free passage over the Dos Casas at a place he was supposed to be guarding? And, what's more, Brenier might, for all Bevan knew, have decided to send out his escaping garrison in penny packets, taking a variety of routes to rejoin the Army of Portugal.

Here we need to consider what Bevan meant in his letter by the phrases 'crossed the river' and 'a patrol from the Portuguese'. The first substantial river Brenier had to cross was the Turon and it is this river one assumes Bevan meant. The place Brenier used must have been roughly two or three miles north-west of Bevan's position, but Bevan does not help us by giving no indication of the time when he first became aware of these enemy troops or how he knew they had crossed the river. One can calculate that Brenier and his two columns reached the Turon around 1.45 am or soon after, and the Dos Casas, three miles or so beyond the Turon, at perhaps 3 am. These suggested timings tally roughly with those put forward by Ward.[13] The French at this stage were travelling west to east, say between one and two miles north of Bevan's Regiment, and going approximately in the direction of Villar de Ciervo. They were being followed, it will be recalled, by Pack's small detachment who were firing at the retreating French. Bevan's men may have heard the noise and for a time wondered if it was the French who were firing, and, if so, whether they were coming towards them, something which might well have contributed to Bevan still deciding to stay put.

A similar element of mystery is attached to this particular Portuguese 'patrol', which has not been mentioned by any of the authorities. We have in the first place to assume that these men came from the Portuguese Dragoons mentioned in Wellington's order of 9 May, apparently under Erskine, and further that they were from one of the dragoon regiments (the 4th and 10th) in Barbacena's Portuguese brigade. It looks as if this detachment was with or close to Bevan and that they came for the moment under his command. It may seem a trifle odd to send this unit, presumably a mounted one, off in the middle of the night to 'reconnoitre' distant Barba del Puerco. It may well be, though this is speculative, that when Bevan received Erskine's orders he felt something had to be done at once. This might have been his method of responding to instructions. The patrol would presumably have left soon after midnight and before Bevan became aware of Brenier's force passing across his front to the north. The Portuguese unit must not be confused with the fifty dragoons from the 1st Royals who were encountered by Brenier a good deal later near Villar de Ciervo. Certainly we do not hear again of Bevan's Portuguese patrol (except that Oman does refer to an unidentified squadron of Barbacena's dragoons arriving at Barba del Puerco from the north-west at the same time as the 36th and 4th).

Whatever the explanation might be, the critical question arising from Bevan's letter of explanation is whether or not the 'reason' he gives for not marching is a convincing one. It seems that Bevan did not deal adequately with the question of why he did not march as soon as he had his orders, late as this might have been. This question is more thoroughly examined in the next chapter. But could there have been any other factor causing him to delay carrying out the order he had received? There is, indeed, another possible explanation for that delay, which came to light many years later in a letter written by Admiral Sir Edward

Fanshawe to the editor of *The Army and Navy Gazette*. Fanshawe, who had been Commander-in-Chief at the North American and West Indian station before becoming Commander-in-Chief at Portsmouth, had written his letter as a result of the publication in 1888 of Stanhope's Conversations with the Duke of Wellington. The Admiral, thinking Bevan had been unfairly treated by the Duke, wrote:

> On Colonel Bevan receiving the order [from Erskine] he said he would do his utmost but he did not know his way through the wood, as he had not been there, and he feared there would be delay in finding a guide at that hour.[14]

As to his source for this information Fanshawe wrote, 'The circumstances were fully related to me some years ago by a very distinguished officer of the highest rank in the Army, who was present and well acquainted with them'.

So was Bevan trying to find at some stage a guide to lead him to Barba del Puerco, but did not wish to mention this to Dunlop? After all, he did use in his letter the words 'a reason'. There could have been more than one. Furthermore, as already mentioned, Colonel Douglas that same night had successfully used guides to reach Barba del Puerco from Junça. It would certainly have made sense for Bevan to be guided seven or eight miles in the dark through unknown country, that is if he could find a reliable guide quickly.

Regarding his delay, Bevan's cause has not been well served by a damaging assertion later made by Wellington to Stanhope. When Bevan received his orders from Erskine, Wellington alleged that 'the people about him said "Oh! You had better not march till daybreak".'[15] This comes close to suggesting that Bevan, unsure of what action he should take, was influenced by his subordinate officers into doing nothing. Oman may have been mindful of Stanhope when he wrote that, because Bevan had received his orders late at night he 'took upon himself the responsibility of

160

ordering that the battalion should only move at daybreak'.[16] Cowper takes the same sort of line in his regimental history: 'There being only a few hours before daybreak, he [Bevan] decided to wait until it was light enough to see his way before going to the Barba del Puerco as directed'.[17]

Bevan reached Barba del Puerco, according to his own account, as we have seen, 'about 6 this morning'. This means that he must therefore have left his station on the Dos Casas at say 3 to 3.30 am to cover the distance of seven to eight miles. What finally induced him to march we cannot be sure. Had he given up waiting for a guide, or had a guide turned up? Or did he feel impelled to move after hearing troops, the French or their pursuers, pass across his front in the direction of Villar de Ciervo? Or perhaps Cowper's simple explanation was the right one. By that time it was, or was becoming, light enough to see his way.[18] At any rate when at last he got moving he and his men must have gone like the wind to reach the bridge. And in the event the 4th came up to the gorge leading down to the river just behind the 36th and were in time to engage the rear of Brenier's columns.

Wellington's response to the escape of the garrison

Wellington made evident to all and sundry his wrath and mortification at what had happened. The news came to him by word of mouth, given by a lieutenant of the 16th Dragoons who had ridden hot foot from the scene. The Commander-in-Chief was also clearly irritated that Campbell had not by mid-morning sent him a report on the events of the night. Typically enough, Wellington lost little time in setting off to Almeida to see the extent of the damage done by Brenier to the fortifications and to gain an idea of how they might be repaired.

In the meantime Dunlop was sending on to Erskine the letter of explanation written on 11 May by Bevan as to why he had delayed in marching. This letter did not reach Colonel Murray at army headquarters until on or after 12 May. Attached to it, no doubt for Wellington's eyes, was a short covering note by Erskine

161

saying that he enclosed Bevan's letter 'accounting for his not marching to Barba del Puerco with his Regiment on the evening of the 10th and as ordered'.[19] The words 'evening' and 'as ordered' were cool in the light of Erskine's long delay in sending on his order to Bevan. When asked by Wellington for an explanation why the bridge at Barba del Puerco was undefended, Erskine said that the 4th Regiment had 'unfortunately missed its way',[20] thereby, or so it seems, covering his own failure to send on Wellington's order promptly. He also told the C-in-C that as soon as he, Erskine, heard explosions at Almeida he sent an officer to ascertain what they were. On receiving a report, he then despatched 'flank battalions' of the 5th Division, which had arrived at Barba del Puerco 'nearly at the same time' as the 4th.[21] Erskine of course wished to show himself in as favourable a light as possible. Wellington accepted what his subordinate had said about the 4th and, a few days later, incorporated Erskine's explanation and comments in his despatches to Liverpool, stating additionally that the enemy were 'saved principally [due] to the unfortunate mistake of the road to Barba del Puerco by the 4th Regiment'.[22]

In his unofficial letter to Liverpool of 15 May, which expanded on his official despatch of the same date, Wellington went further when saying, 'If they [the 4th] had not missed their road to Barba del Puerco the garrison must have laid down their arms'.[23] This statement might be considered overconfident since it took no account of the French battalions on the eastern bank of the Agueda sent there by Reynier to assist Brenier in making his crossing by the bridge. Also, earlier in the same unofficial letter Wellington was inaccurate when he said 'I believe we have taken or destroyed the greatest part of the garrison'. This of course was an ill-founded estimate, at least partly based, presumably, on Campbell's over-optimistic report. In fact Brenier's losses were some 25% of his force.

Yet was there any truth in Erskine's allegation that the 4th lost its way? Admiral Fanshawe's statement that Bevan 'did not know his way through the wood' has been referred to above and also to

162

the possibility that he had sought a guide, but there is no reason to believe Bevan ever lost his way at any stage. Certainly no one else ever suggested that the 4th were lost. Indeed the contemporary diarist Tomkinson specifically contradicts Erskine, commenting that 'it was not the case' that the 4th missed its way.[24] One of Wellington's biographers, Maxwell, seems to endorse this view. In addition Hercules Pakenham told his father that 'Campbell [Longford says he meant Erskine] unjustly threw the Slur of having lost his way' on Bevan of the 4th.[25] It is not unreasonable to conclude that the story put about by Erskine was just plainly false.

In accepting what Erskine had told him, there is no evidence that Wellington summoned Bevan to hear his side of the story. That of course may not have been the Commander-in-Chief's method. On the other hand Wellington certainly did hear from someone that the 4th Regiment had not got its orders until around midnight. This, however, clearly did not cut any ice with him as he was under the mistaken impression that the 4th was located only two and a half miles, and not as we calculate seven to eight miles, from Barba del Puerco, and should therefore easily have got to the place in time. Wellington's contention that the distance to be covered was two and a half miles got into his unofficial letter to Lord Liverpool.[26] This error was unfortunately repeated by others, relying on what Wellington had told Liverpool. Thus Oman refers to this distance (in a footnote only), while Fortescue adopts the distance in his main text. Also, Longford says Bevan 'had under 3 miles to go'. Curiously enough, and showing how inconsistent even a great commander can be, in his 'Conversations' with Stanhope Wellington said, 'I had stationed him [Bevan] six miles' from the bridge. The extent to which Wellington had got his knife into Bevan over the episode is further illustrated in these Conversations when he said, baldly enough, that the escape of the French garrison was 'the fault of our Colonel Bevan'.[27] He included no one else. At least this is the impression gained from what Stanhope reported. It was as if the unfortunate Bevan, *per*

Wellington, had been single-handedly responsible for Brenier and his 1000 men reaching safety across the Agueda River.

As far as Wellington was concerned he had told the story of the Almeida garrison in his despatches and that, for him, was the end of the matter. He never afterwards deviated from the account he gave Liverpool. Bevan in fact became for him the scapegoat for the army's failure, and in his eyes would always remain so. Of course at this stage in the middle of May Bevan had no idea, as far as we are aware, of the line Wellington was taking.

As for the other principal actors in the drama of the night of 10/11 May Campbell was particularly lucky to escape censure, but then he was a friend of the Prince Regent. On the other hand Wellington never again entrusted him with an important task. The recalcitrant Cochrane, however, got a stinging rebuke for his ill-advised pursuit of the French which led to Wellington's well-known remark that 'there is nothing so stupid as a gallant officer'.[28] Later Cochrane was court-martialled, though not for his conduct at Barba del Puerco. The inactive Iremonger was tireless in defending his reputation, but, surprisingly, received, as far as is known, no criticism from Wellington.

The apportionment of blame for the disaster by the two classical historians of the war is interesting. William Napier picked out Campbell and Erskine for censure (his brother General Sir Charles Napier reversed the order), while Oman blamed Erskine and Iremonger, and to a lesser extent Campbell for how he had disposed of his troops. Fortescue, whose history of the British army covers the Peninsular wars in great detail, believed a great many officers were to blame, Campbell probably most of all.[29]

Ward's article on Brenier's Escape
A well researched and carefully argued article was written nearly half a century ago for the *Journal of the Society for Army Historical Research* by S.G.P.Ward, entitled 'Brenier's escape from Almeida, 1811'.[30] This is probably the best and most authoritative account of Brenier's escape. Ward concludes his article very reasonably by

laying the main blame for the escape on Campbell, who had not, Ward considered, adequately arranged his blockading forces, nor strengthened his picket lines. Ward also takes a hefty swipe at the inactivity of Iremonger.

As for the 4th Foot, Ward stated that the movements of that Regiment 'do not seem to me the principal feature in the escape of the garrison'. The estimated '400 men' of the 4th could not be expected to meet 'head on and intercept unaided, 1400 desperate Frenchmen'. He thought its role should have been regarded more as a 'large outlying picket'. He does, however, emphasize that Bevan could have reached Barba del Puerco without difficulty by 'two or three' in the morning if he had started at midnight when ordered to.[31]

Ward paid special attention to Bevan's letter to Dunlop, and commented: 'His explanation cannot be altogether believed.' Yet he dealt with Bevan's predicament sympathetically, pointing out, perhaps rather generously, that Bevan would have been used to the Quartermaster-General's orders coming out in the evening for execution the following morning. Thus he feels that Bevan might have had a 'genuine misunderstanding of them' or 'an understandable reluctance to rouse his men'. On the other hand, as we know, Bevan was not unused to being called out at night. In a letter written to Mary just three weeks before Bevan mentioned that the 4th had been called out at half past twelve at night. (see p.131) This was something which Ward would not have known about, as he had no knowledge of Bevan's correspondence.

One must be in broad agreement with what Ward wrote, except that he lets Erskine off too lightly. Certainly it was fair comment for him to write that it was 'too easy to follow the fashion and blame Erskine' for the Almeida disaster. But, in assessing Erskine as a soldier, Ward disregards his blunders at Casal Nova and Sabugal, and ignores or plays down the defects in his character and his instability.

A balanced view needs to be taken over the question of allied responsibility for the Almeida disaster. Fortescue must be right when he concluded that a 'great number of officers were to blame' for it. However Erskine and his role in the affair is perceived, it is nonetheless difficult to believe that had Bevan, and one is by no means trying to whitewash the part he played, received his orders at say 6 pm on 10 May the story of Brenier's escape would have been a different one. For then Bevan would surely have marched and been in place in the vicinity of the bridge hours before Brenier's arrival there. The 4th Foot, and others, might not have been wholly successful in stopping the French, but then Brenier would never have got 1000 men back across the bridge to rejoin the Army of Portugal.

CHAPTER FOURTEEN

And so to Portalegre

What of Bevan's own reaction to the events of the night of 10/11 May? To Mary he had alluded to them in the briefest fashion. It goes without saying that he must have been disgusted when he soon heard, as he must have done, that Erskine had sat on Wellington's order of 10 May for many hours. Bevan was a conscientious officer and would have been horrifed at Erskine's casualness. He could hardly not have felt badly let down by his divisional commander. Never, though, in the letters he wrote to Mary after 11 May is there any sort of reference, disparaging or otherwise, to Erskine. He did, however, as we have seen, feel obliged on 11 May – or was he required to make a report? – to account for his late arrival at the bridge at Barba del Puerco. But did he in that report furnish Dunlop with the full reasons? As noted the historian Ward was dubious about this, and one is bound to share his doubts.

Given what is known about the movement of French and allied troops that night and given, in addition, that one's various conjectures concerning them, especially in regard to the 4th Foot, are reasonable, to what extent, if at all, did Bevan perceive himself to blame for Brenier's escape by not being at the bridge? On this one can only speculate. Certainly at this stage there is no evidence to suggest that Bevan was aware that Wellington was going to pin the responsibility for the escape on the 4th. In defending his action that night to his superiors it may well be that Bevan genuinely believed what he did was correct in the circumstances. After the tardy arrival of his orders from Erskine was it not too late, he could well have argued, to blunder off in the middle of the night trying to find that very distant bridge? And then how exactly was he to guard it? Yet, no fool, Bevan must have realized, if he had paused to reflect, the tactical importance of the bridge. He would, therefore, hardly have been human if he did not at the same time have some niggling worries about his not being there, as ordered, to ensure its proper defence.

The position on the Agueda-Azaba front before Ciudad Rodrigo having changed as a result of Marmont withdrawing his forces to the east, Wellington ordered the 3rd and 7th Divisions south to help Beresford on the Elvas-Badajoz front. On 16 May he himself left his Vila Formoso headquarters and rode off at his usual furious speed to visit Beresford, leaving Spencer in charge, having given him instructions on the defensive role he was to assume, and on when and how he was to retire should any reemergant French force decide to advance. Wellington arrived at Elvas on 19 May, three days too late for the bloody Battle of Albuera in which Beresford, though with heavy losses, got the better of Soult, who consequently was forced to retreat south-east towards the mountains and Seville. In this situation the Commander-in-Chief thought the moment opportune to try and reduce the important fortress of Badajoz still held by the French. Wellington himself took charge of the siege operations, but the absence of sufficient heavy artillery and the strength of the forts frustrated allied efforts, persistent as they were. So, with no progress made, Wellington decided on 10 June to abandon his exertions before Badajoz and to retire west across the broad Guadiana to the line Elvas-Campo Maior, taking up his headquarters by 20 June at the Quinta Sao Jaoa roughly between these two places.

Another important factor contributing to his decision to disengage related to the movements of the French. Marmont, with commendable energy and efficiency, had reorganized the Army of Portugal after Masséna's departure and, as anticipated by Wellington, had early in June begun marching south with 30,000 men to assist Soult, though not before he had sallied out from Ciudad Rodrigo with a modest force to make a demonstration in the direction of Almeida, a move which gave the brave but not very able Spencer an initial fright. For his part Soult, recovering from his defeat at Albuera, had moved north again, and at Merida on 18 June joined forces with Marmont. Their combined army, numbering a formidable 60,000 men, proceded west towards Badajoz ready again to challenge the allies.

During the second half of May Bevan and his regiment, still part of the 5th Division, remained in the north as part of Spencer's force watching the French across the Azaba, although the 4th had moved some miles south from Aldea de Obispo to the village of Nave de Aver, which Bevan disliked and called a 'vile' place. From here, having been afforded much 'happiness' by receiving two letters from his wife, he wrote on 28 May to Mary in cheerful mood singing the praises of Wellington. 'Often people in England,' he wrote, 'do not do justice to the merit of Lord Wellington,' who had 'most admirably performed his duty'.[1] These remarks provide evidence that up to this date Bevan had no inkling that Wellington was blaming the 4th for the disaster at Barba del Puerco. If somehow, perhaps from the staff, Bevan had had advance knowledge of the contents of Wellington's despatch of 15 May he would hardly have written in these terms to Mary.

As the centre of operations against the French was now shifting to the south Wellington wanted his troops left in the north to join him on the Elvas-Campo Maior front. So, Spencer, who had already been obliged to release two brigades for service in the south, began in June to move the rest of his force south through Alfayates and Sabugal, the latter place being reached by Bevan on 10 June.

During his march south Bevan, in his surviving letters to Mary, refers constantly to his family, about whom Mary gave regular news. Thus we hear through Charles' pen how Mary dined with his cousin, the faithful Mrs Shaw; about the debt Charles the younger owed his mother for her kind attention on some undisclosed matter; of Tom's aversion to study which his father sensibly

169

thought was quite natural (the poor little chap was only four and a half years old!) and about Bevan's mother and her continued indecisiveness about where to live. Also, he reported that Paterson had commanded the 28th at the Battle of Albuera and had acquitted himself with credit. There was not a lot in his letters about the march except to refer to the 'ghastly' heat, but on 19 June at Castelo Branco Charles wrote in the context of the reappearance of Soult and his forces in the south, that 'Lord Wellington knows how to deal with' the French.[2] Up to this moment Bevan appeared to retain his high regard for the Commander-in-Chief.

The route after Castelo Branco lay south down to Vila Velha on the Tagus, which the 4th crossed on 22 June, and on to the attractive town of Portalegre. The 4th regimental history contains a descriptive passage about that long June march and how in the evenings a camp would be set up usually on the edge of a wood near a stream. After each battalion had provided companies for picket duty

> the rest of the battalion set to work to make the camp. Arms were piled; the wood resounded with the blows of axes and bill-hooks, the stones were fetched to make fire-places where the women prepared and cooked the food. The officers would lie apart under the trees, their swords hanging in the branches above them and their dogs crouching by their sides. The light of twenty fires would be reflected on the stands of piled arms, and the men enveloped in their great-coats, sitting or lying round them would talk over the events of the day and every now and then break into a laugh or a song.[3]

This report makes campaigning against Napoleon's forces in Iberia sound, just for a moment, like an idyll! Finally, the Light, 5th and 6th Divisions came to rest some 13 miles beyond Portalegre at Arronches, reached by the 4th Foot on 24 June. These divisions Wellington held, for the present, in reserve and behind the Elvas-Campo Maior front line.

Bevan and his Regiment had reached Arronches at a time of rising tension along the front, which lasted for about a week. This tension was due of course to the conjunction of the massive French forces which, as we have recounted, had swept up to and beyond Badajoz. Napier calls the moment as being 'one of the most dangerous of the whole war'.[4]

But in the event the two French marshals, Soult and Marmont, on learning from reconnaissances that the whole Anglo-Portuguese army was in front of them and remembering their recent defeats at the hands of Wellington, were not disposed to make any kind of attack despite their numerical superiority. In fact Soult, receiving news of an insurrection in southern Andalusia and being concerned about the security of Seville in his rear, proceeded at this moment to leave the front line with most of his troops. As a result the time of immediate danger for the allies passed. Nevertheless, even up to the middle of July, the opposing forces stood warily observing each other from the different sides of the Guadiana River.

There had by now reached Bevan a highly disagreeable piece of news and just at a time perhaps when the events at Barba del Puerco were beginning to recede from his immediate memory. Sometime in the second half of June *The London Gazette*, as well as other newspapers, had arrived in Portugal containing in its columns Wellington's official despatch of 15 May to Lord Liverpool about the escape of the Almeida garrison. For the first time the army at the front now learnt exactly what Wellington had reported to the War Minister about the affair and perceived that he had placed the main blame for the disaster at Barca del Puerco on the 4th Regiment, and therefore on Bevan. It is well to repeat what he said. After referring to the French attack on the allied pickets and how the enemy 'were well guided between the positions occupied by our troops', Wellington went on:

The 4th Regiment which was ordered to occupy Barba del Puerco, unfortunately missed the road, and did not arrive there till the Enemy had reached the Place, and commenced to descend the Bridge . . . The enemy are indebted for the small (sic) part of the garrison which they have saved principally to the unfortunate mistake of the road to Barba del Puerco by the 4th Regiment.[5]

There was also the equally damning unofficial letter written by Wellington to Liverpool on 15 May in which he stated the 4th had only 'two and a half miles to march' and that 'if they had not missed the road, the garrison must have laid down their arms'. Even if this letter was not published, its contents were likely to have become known to the army. The English newspapers too were full of discussion about the escape of the French and one of the jingles appearing ran as follows:

> The Lion went to sleep
> And the Lambs were at play.
> The eagle spread his wings
> And from Almeida flew away.[6]

The 'Lion' was the 4th Foot and the 'Lambs' the 2nd Foot.

We do not know when precisely Bevan first read Wellington's stinging words but it must have been sometime after he had passed through Castelo Branco. His reaction to what he read was predictable enough. He considered that what the Commander-in-Chief had reported was plainly inaccurate. His regiment had not 'missed' the road, or, in other words, got lost. Nor was his regiment 'principally' to blame for the enemy who had escaped. Angry and shocked, he felt a terrible slur had been cast on the good name of the Regiment and on himself. Further, Wellington's allegations and conclusions were taken by Bevan as being an affront to his military capability and even to his personal honour. There was much to put right and, as he must have seen it, little time to lose. Already in the army some lively discussion must have developed and the reputation of the 4th was consequently in question. So Bevan decided to apply at once to Wellington for an inquiry. This was a logical and understandable course to follow, for at an inquiry he could be heard and explain his actions. Whether or not he consulted his superiors about this application is not known. There would have been no point in going to Erskine and in any case that officer had been moved by Wellington by 25 June to another appointment. He could have gone to Dunlop – his application would of course have had to be sent through his brigadier – but Dunlop never seems to be mentioned by contemporaries or historians. There is a hint once in Bevan's letters that Dunlop liked his creature comforts, but as to his qualities as a commander or superior we are ignorant.

Most historians have maintained that it was an enquiry that Bevan applied for, but Major Hercules Pakenham, who, because his brother Edward was then Assistant Adjutant General and might have been expected to have had some inside knowledge, stated that Bevan had asked for an investigation.[7] On the other hand Elizabeth Longford put a rather different slant on the affair, writing that Wellington, while realizing that Bevan had received Erskine's orders late, considered that this did not excuse Bevan's delay. This was because the C-in-C thought wrongly that Bevan had only a short distance to go to the bridge. She went on:

He [Wellington] turned down Bevan's request for an inquiry into the respective responsibilities of himself and Erskine deciding instead to bring Bevan before a court-martial.[8]

The word 'responsibilities' is puzzling, as we do not hear elsewhere that any kind of a problem existed between the two men in this area. Perhaps a request couched in this way was a device to bring into the open Erskine's failure on the night of 10/11 May. Only one other source has referred to a court-martial. This was James Dacres, Bevan's brother-in-law, who said many years later that

Bevan had 'directly applied for a court-martial or enquiry'.[9] We may note that Longford would not have had access to what Dacres had written.

Bevan was, or had been, an admirer of Wellington and so must have been optimistic that his request for an inquiry would be granted and that as a result of it the Commander-in-Chief would accept that the main blame for Brenier's escape could not with justice be placed on the shoulders of the 4th Foot. As Bevan awaited the outcome of his application he would have been rehearsing what he might say in presenting his case. What were the chief points? For a start there were a number of facts to be emphasized or put right. For instance he had received his orders from Erskine very late indeed. Then he had not 'missed the road' or got lost. A sensitive man, he felt strongly about this. Further, he and his Regiment had to travel some seven or eight miles through unknown territory, much of it wooded broken country, and not the two and a half miles as Wellington seemed to imagine was the distance.

But above all he needed to explain convincingly why he did not march as soon as he had received his orders. On this fundamental matter his explanatory letter written on 11 May, he might have seen in retrospect, was not adequate. He could of course point out that when he first heard the French soldiery that night – we have set the time at about 1.45 a.m. – he thought they might be approaching his position on the Dos Casas, and that accordingly he did not wish for tactical reasons to vacate his post at that moment. This, however, would not have gone to the root of the question, for he had received his belated orders from Erskine some one and three-quarter hours earlier. What had he been doing during that time? Of course, if Bevan had had a genuine misunderstanding about his orders, as postulated by the historian Ward (see p 165) – and their precise wording would be critical – this would be an important factor in any inquiry.

On the question of broad responsibility for Brenier's escape perhaps he could be bold enough to remonstrate about the failure of the other allied troops in the cordon to stop the French. This was a central issue but it would be a brave man who mentioned it in the circumstances.

These were all reasonable points to make, but just what weight would they carry and would he succeed, when basing his case on them, in attaining his object, that is of removing the slur from his regiment's name and from his own?

Finally in an inquiry, and this was something no one, however confident, could afford to overlook, other points embarrassing for him might emerge. These could include the accusations that he was reluctant to disturb his already bedded-down men, or was swayed by poor advice from subordinates, or was unwilling to move without a guide or even was plain indecisive. These sort of questions might have made him wonder if he had used his discretion wisely that night, and if he should not, after all, have marched for the bridge as soon as he had his orders, whatever the difficulties there were lying in his way. Indeed, at worst, he might have begun to believe that the 4th Foot had let the army down. And if this were so, whose responsibility was it? There could only be one answer.

Unhappily Bevan had misjudged Wellington. The Commander-in-Chief, with plenty else on his mind, had no intention of reopening a matter on which he had committed himself weeks before. Bevan's request for an inquiry was refused. James Dacres, again writing many years after, mentioned that the refusal to hold an inquiry was made 'dismissively', Wellington taking the view the escape of the garrison was 'somebody's fault'.[10] In other words he had decided it was Bevan's and that was that.

Bevan was stunned by Wellington's refusal to grant him a hearing, disbelief soon turning to despair. His and his Regiment's honour was still at stake. From all sides this conscientious man was assailed by dread and doubt. How could he now look the world in the face? Would the Regiment continue to respect him? Should he resign? Or was there some other course of action open to him? These were among the thoughts which must have gnawed at his very soul.

On 2 July the 4th moved north from Arronches to Portalegre. Two days later Bevan wrote a letter to Mary, to which reference was made in the Prologue. The text, which is prosaic enough, is quoted in full:

We are once more, My dearest Mary, on the march but for what place we are entirely ignorant, and are now waiting for orders whither to proceed – Some people think we are to remain here but I fear this is too good a place for the Fifth Division – I imagine our movements depend totally on those of the Enemy, therefore I have no doubt but they will contrive to give us trouble enough – The weather is terribly hot and very uncomfortable, our men feel the effects of it, indeed so do most of the Regts, in a greater or less degree.

I had the pleasure to receive your letter of the 17th, I hope you are all quite well for you say only pretty well: but I know you never conceal from me anything of this kind. I therefore am so far satisfied. I should be most unhappy was I left to torment myself with constant apprehension on this account – I am much afraid you will [have] trouble or rather diffi- culty enough in procuring a house for my Mother – Col Williams is now here and quite recovered from the wound he received at the Battle of Fuentes D'Onoro. He also informed me that the Montague Square house was to be disposed of.

What is to become of all of us I know not, but suppose we shall linger out the summer and in the latter part of the year the French will either bring reinforcements or evacuate the country – I was just going to see Paterson when we received an order to march – and God knows now when I may have another opportunity – I have only one horse that I can ride and he has a sore back, so I am not able to make many distant excursions. I have an opportunity to send this letter im- mediately and having really nothing to tell you but that I am very much fatigued and very anxious to hear that all at Money

Hill are well, I shall conclude by begging my best love to all your party – and many blessings for yourself and Children

God protect you my beloved Mary
I am always yours   C.B.
    I will write to Caroline in a day or two.[11]

By the time Bevan wrote this letter he would certainly have applied to Wellington for an inquiry but might not have known the result of his application. He mentions nothing of all this to Mary, nor is there any hint to her of the turmoil through which he must have been going, except that he does say he was 'very much fatigued'. In the past he had quite frequently, as we have seen, shared worries with Mary. Not now. This was something from which she had to be shielded. There is, however, the clear indication of how his wish to see his brother-in-law, Jim Paterson, had been frustrated by events. Very likely he had wanted to talk over with him the awful predicament in which he now found himself. From Paterson he could have expected sympathy, and sound advice. But his brother-in-law was many miles away serving with his regiment in the 1st Division in the centre of the front line. Who else could he turn to? There seemed no close friend, no trusted senior officer who might fit the bill. Would that, for instance, Edward Paget was at hand to give him counsel.

Bevan did not take Wellington's refusal as being his final word and, according to Dacres, repeated his application.[12] And it is possible, although this is speculative, that he may even have sought an interview with the, at this moment, peripatetic Wellington. But the Iron Duke, as he was to become known, was not to be moved.

There can be little doubt that for Bevan his old enemies, the Blue Devils, like the Furies, had now returned to torment him, swirling round and round with a vengeance. Agonisingly he plunged into a black hole of depression in which Mary and the children were light years away, and played, alas, no shadow of a part in influencing his actions. In his distress and confusion he kept returning to his responsibility as commanding officer of his Regiment and of ensuring that its high reputation was maintained. He had tried and now failed to have the stain cast upon its good name removed. This failure added to his feelings that he was now disgraced. As he came to see it there was one way, and one way only, in which a man of honour could atone for the shame surrounding him and his Regiment.

Alone and utterly disconsolate, on 8 July in his quarters at Portalegre Bevan made his decision to put an end to his misery. Before he shot himself he left a note for Paterson. In it he explained his military character was tarnished.[13]

CHAPTER FIFTEEN

Aftermath

The funeral of Charles Bevan took place with all the military honours due to his rank at Portalegre two days after his death. For the occasion Major John Piper, Charles' second in command, issued the following order:

> The Battalion will parade at a quarter before 12 o'clock. No one to be absent (sick & public batmen excepted) as the funeral of the late Lt Col Bevan will take place at that hour, when the Officers will assemble at Major Piper's quarters as mentioned in the division order yesterday. A firing party consisting of four Capts 8 Subalterns & 300 rank & file under command of Major Tanner will be ready, for the purpose of showing (in conjunction with other Officers of the Division who may attend) the last sad respect to the remains of their late justly esteemed and deeply lamented Commander.[1]

After his burial in the yard of Portalegre castle, Bevan's grave was bricked over and a stone, suitably inscribed, placed at its head. In a note written for the Bevan family Piper referred to the 'high estimation in which his character was held by all who had the good fortune of enjoying either his friendship or acquaintance.' Piper had been, he assured the family, on the best of terms with his commanding officer, whose loss he deeply deplored.[2] No doubt this was the kind of tribute which might have been expected in the circumstances, and it would have been of some comfort to Mary.

The Regiment had, after the funeral was over, the usual dismal matters to attend to such as the sale of Bevan's effects, which Mary was later told had brought in £300. Some items, his sword, watch, compass, writing-book and a trunk in due course found their way back to England. In settling the affairs of his friend and brother-in-law, Paterson, coming back from his place at the front, took a leading part.

The army was shocked at Bevan's death and the circumstances surrounding it. 'Public opinion in the army,' wrote Oman, 'held that he [Bevan] has been sacrificed to the hierarchical theory that a general must be believed before a lieutenant-colonel.' The contemporary diarists Simmons and Tomkinson, both members of Wellington's army, wrote sympathetically about what had happened to Bevan. Similarly the regimental history commented that 'he was a good officer and had the sympathy of the whole army'.[3] Years later Mary's brother, James Dacres, told his nephew, young Charles Bevan, that 'Every officer there considered your father a very ill-used man,' but he had, Dacres said, 'the most romantic ideas of military honour'.[4] A hundred and ninety years on, this author has not found any evidence of a contemporary diarist, soldier or historian taking a view other than a sympathetic one towards Bevan and his untimely end. The exception seems to have been the Duke of Wellington.

It is not possible to write of Bevan's death without expressing some thoughts about the part Wellington played in the whole affair and how that great commander of armies emerges as a manager of men. The question is raised in the first place because Bevan's death might have been prevented with a modicum of sound man management. Why then did Wellington refuse to allow Bevan any sort of hearing or inquiry? Was it connected in any way with wishing to protect Erskine, or even Campbell? There may be something in such an idea, for Longford suggested that there was an element of fatalism in Wellington's character. He had tried and failed, she argued, to get rid of Erskine. So nothing would be achieved by telling the world that one of his generals had lapses through taking too much liquor.[5] Or was it more likely that he obstinately did not wish to reopen, on whatever grounds, a sore matter nearly two months old? Never liking to admit he was in the wrong, he had already gone into print on the subject of the blame for Brenier's escape and he would not go back on what he had reported.

In fact Wellington did not have a good reputation regarding his treatment of subordinates. Unlike, say, Sir John Moore, he was not a loveable character, and writers have accused him over the years, with some justification, of carelessness with other people's feelings. Recently the historian Andrew Roberts has expanded on this theme by citing some examples. Sir Charles Stewart, Adjutant-General, was reduced to tears by the Commander-in-Chief's hectoring. Dr McGrigor, chief of Wellington's medical staff and a man who made a significant contribution to improving medical care in the Peninsular War, was once unfairly berated by Wellington after explaining the arrangements made for the care of the sick and wounded. At Vitoria Captain Norman Ramsay moved the position of his battery when he should have remained where he was. This happened owing to a muddle over orders, something which was not Ramsay's fault. Wellington, incensed, was determined to make an example of him and so had him placed under arrest for three weeks. Then there was Lieutenant-Colonel Sturgeon, who, severely reprimanded for not obtaining a guide, sought to redeem himself by purposely galloping straight into the midst of enemy skirmishers and being shot in the head. There was also the case, not mentioned by Roberts, of Major Alexander Todd of the Royal Staff Corps. According to the Rev G.R.Gleig, who knew Wellington well and was in the 1840s Chaplain-General to the Forces, Major Todd, son of a butler, was rebuked by Wellington when a bridge he had built fell down in the winter of 1813/14. Harshly, Wellington refused to accept excuses and rudely asked Todd whether he was going to take up his father's trade. Todd, overcome, deliberately placed himself the following day in a place where he could scarcely avoid French marksmen. He fell, riddled with musket balls. The truth of Gleig's story about Todd has recently been strongly disputed in a learned journal.[6] We may well take the view that Wellington's failure to deal sensibly with Bevan's request was inexcusable, but it was not perhaps atypical of the man.

*　　*　　*　　*

A decision was quickly made at Portalegre, with Jim Paterson taking the lead and being supported by Piper, to do all that was possible to conceal the true cause of Bevan's death from Mary Bevan and her immediate family. Wellington's headquarters must have concurred in this course of action. A formula was accordingly devised by Paterson which would, it was hoped, satisfy Mary. The 'story', which is referred in the Prologue, was that Bevan had suddenly gone down with a terrible fever and within a few days had succumbed to it. There was still much fever around in the army, some of it a hangover from the Scheldt expedition, as we have seen in these pages, so this could be a plausible explanation for his sudden death.

Within three days of Charles' death, Paterson had written two letters to Colonel Henry Torrens, the Military Secretary at Horse Guards, giving him the facts behind the tragedy and the proposal for a cover-up. On 29 July – this shows the speed at which the army could operate administratively when it needed to – Torrens replied to Paterson with notable sensitivity and helpfulness:

> I assure you I very much deplore the melancholy event of poor Colonel Bevan's death. No person can feel more forcibly than myself the extent of misery into which a family is thrown by the untimely and unexpected occurrence of the death of a father and a husband aggravated by the shocking circumstances which have attended it! I trust the real story may be concealed effectually and permanently from the immediate family of Col. B. Yet the occasion of his death is

so universally known and talked of that I fear it will be difficult to conceal the truth . . .'[7]

Furthermore, Torrens would, as necessary, 'frame a story consistent with what you have given out in your letters', and promised not to mention the 'requests' in the suicide note left for Paterson. We have no idea what these requests might have been. In addition to Jim Paterson's initiative, his wife Eleanor had written before the end of July on behalf of her distraught sister, asking for 'particulars' of Charles' death. Torrens had also responded promptly to this letter. There is evidence that Jim Paterson knew Torrens quite well;[8] if this were so, his wife might not have been inhibited from writing to quite a senior figure in the army hierarchy in London.

There was another important matter raised by Torrens in his letter to Paterson, a matter which Torrens had in fact already addressed to the Commander-in-Chief of the Army, the Duke of York. This concerned the sale of Charles Bevan's Lieutenant-Colonelcy, which, it will be recalled, had been purchased by him only about eighteen months before his death. It would seem from Torrens' letter that the Duke of York did 'not consider himself justified in admitting the sale of the Lt-Colonelcy', but once Mrs Bevan had established her right to a pension, the Duke would 'appropriate a Company to be sold for her benefit'. In other words, she would receive a sum for a Captaincy, but not for Charles' Lieutenant-Colonelcy. The mention of a 'pension' is interesting. By committing suicide an officer might well have been forfeiting any right his wife had to a pension. But when the army, as had happened in the case of Bevan, appeared to acknowledge another quite different cause of death, then it would presumably be unable to deny the widow a pension.

James Dacres was serving on his ship on the North American station at the time of Charles' death and so could not lend the Dacres family his support in person at a critical moment; he could only write to his sister to express his sorrow. Back on leave in England in the autumn, Dacres again wrote, this time on

11 October, to Mary,[9] who was in Norfolk. She, still confused by what had happened in Portugal, had asked her brother for his help in getting certain matters clarified. For, despite the best endeavours of the Patersons, both Jim and Eleanor, and no doubt others, there was still information about Charles' death – from fever as she believed the cause to be – which Mary lacked. For instance, she wanted to know whether religious rites had been available to Charles, or whether he had any trusted servant with him. She had also asked for the name of the surgeon. These were, of course, impossible questions for her brother to answer, but he did his best to comfort her. He could only relay, as he told her, what Piper had said, viz, 'no attention of any kind was wanting either to soothe or relieve his feelings'. And no one, James stressed to his sister, was better loved or respected than her husband. Mary, as far as we know, did not suspect that the true cause of Charles' death was being concealed from her, in spite of the dissembling which now, of necessity, went on.

The cover up, which was to cause the Bevans and Dacres some problems in the years ahead, was primarily designed for Mary's peace of mind and to protect her children. The plan seems to have succeeded, despite Torrens' misgivings, certainly as far as Mary and the children were concerned, and there is some evidence to suggest that Mary was still unaware of Charles' suicide 32 years after the event. The probability is that she died in ignorance of it. But sooner rather than later Mrs Dacres senior, Mary's mother, knew the full story, as did her daughters Eleanor and Jemima. It was, therefore, even more remarkable that her close family was able to shield Mary from the true facts for all those years

In time James Dacres thought his nephew Charles Bevan, who was about to go up to Balliol, Oxford, should hear about his father's death. Somehow the true story had never reached him at school at Charterhouse. Somebody would be needed to provide the necessary enlightenment, and James thought it should be one of his sisters. For some reason he was not suggesting himself for the task. But just then old Mrs Dacres, in her seventies, intervened, put her foot down strongly against the course of action being proposed and, furthermore, chided her son James for even considering it. The time, she said, was not ripe. Now, at the end of her life, she was anxious to let sleeping dogs lie. When the appropriate moment for revealing the truth did one day come, she thought her daughter Eleanor was the 'properest person to do it', as she was very fond of her nephew, though Mrs Dacres did not rule out Jemima. She was also shocked that James had mentioned to young Charles the army as a possible career for him. This was quite wrong as Mary had planned a legal career for him and had been 'scraping every shilling she could save to enable her to give him an education for it'. The last thing old Mrs Dacres wished for was 'misery and discord' in the family.[10]

So, strong character that she was, Mrs Dacres had her way about the family secret and about Charles' career. But family secrets, as is their wont, have a habit of emerging into the open. Nearly 20 years later Charles, by then a practising barrister on the Western circuit, wrote to his uncle. He told him that he had recently learnt 'my father put an end to his life and that the shocking event was mainly attributable to some real or imagined disgrace brought upon himself and his Corps at the time of the evacuation of Almeida by the French.' He further expressed a wish to know plainly whether 'his father was in the opinion of competent judges culpable or not,' while he and his brothers, he emphasized, were ready to make further inquiries if need be.[11]

By return his uncle wrote him a long and kindly letter telling him what really happened at Portalegre and why his father had taken his own life. Moreover, he assured his nephew, 'Not the slightest blame was thrown upon his character by military men, or any person who knew the circumstances'. As for the aftermath of Bevan's death, 'In the excitement of an active and bloody campaign the thing was dropt without any notice, by the Horse Guards, the Duke [Wellington] then beginning to be all powerful'. He also mentioned that the circumstances of his father's death was one of the reasons why his grandmother and aunts had 'always objected to any of you going into the army'.[12]

Charles Bevan junior went on to have a successful career in the law, in due course becoming a county court judge in Cornwall. He was also a part-time soldier serving as a Captain in the 13th Duke of Cornwall's Artillery. His obituarist wrote in 1872 that he 'was noted for his hospitality and agreeable and genial manners. The very appearance of his happy smiling face was a cure for melancholy, and he consequently enjoyed considerable popularity and possessed a wide circle of friends'.[13] It is a relief to know that the father did not seem to have handed down to the son his fatal tendency to harbour 'Blue Devils'. Certainly Charles senior would have been proud of his eldest son and his accomplishments.

Thomas, the second son, became a parson and was in time Vicar of Twickenham. He married and in true Victorian style his wife, another Mary, bore him ten children. One of his granddaughters was Georgina whose novel about Charles Bevan has played a part in this history. A great grandson of Thomas, Major James Bevan, renewed the family association with the 4th Foot, the King's Own Royal Regiment. He was commissioned into that regiment in 1913, fought in the First World War and inherited Charles Bevan's sword. In the course of time that sword was presented by the family to the regimental museum at Lancaster. Edward, the third and youngest son, continued the tradition of his mother's family, by joining the Royal Navy, and died unmarried in his mid 50s. As for little Eleanor, whom her father never saw, she grew up to marry a parson with a living in Yorkshire, but there is no record of her having had a family.

Envoi

As the years passed the story of Charles Bevan was not forgotten by his descendants. His letters were carefully preserved and in time were used, as we have seen, as source material for the novel Georgina Bevan wrote about her great-grandfather. Her nephew, Major James Bevan, did not neglect to pass on the history of Charles to his daughter Anne, and Anne in turn retold it to her husband William Colfer.

In 1999 William Colfer, now a widower, visited Portugal to try and locate Charles Bevan's grave. He made a thorough search in the area around Portalegre castle and its ruins, but despite considerable help from the municipality and local people, his efforts were in vain. Of the grave there was no visible sign.

With the agreement of the Portuguese authorities, the King's Own Royal Border Regiment and members of the Bevan family, William Colfer arranged for a replacement memorial stone to his late wife's ancestor to be placed in the British military cemetery at Elvas. A simple ceremony took place there on 14 October 2000 to dedicate the memorial stone to Charles Bevan. The ceremony was attended by representatives of the Portuguese army, the British Embassy at Lisbon, the King's Own Royal Border Regiment, including the commanding officer of the battalion then serving in Kosovo, the British Historical Society of Portugal, the Friends of Elvas cemetery and by descendants of Charles Bevan. The memorial stone was inscribed with the following words:

This stone is erected to the memory of Charles Bevan, late Lieut.Col. of the 4th or King's Own Regt, with the intention of recording his virtues. They are deeply engraved on the hearts of those who knew him and will ever live in their remembrance.

A stone with this inscription was erected over the grave of Col Bevan in Portalegre Castle where he was buried on 11 July 1811. That stone having been removed when a road was built there, this replacement is placed by his descendants to honour the memory of an officer who put regimental honour before his own life.

Notes

Prologue
1. Bevan Papers, Charles (C)-Mary (M), in early April, but undated, 1811
2. ibid, C-M, 9 May, 1811
3. ibid, C-M, 10 June, 1811
4. ibid, C-M, 19 June, 1811
5. ibid, C-M, 4 July, 1811
6. ibid, J.R. Dacres – M, 15 October, 1811
7. ibid

Chapter 1
1. Richard Holmes, *Redcoat*, London, HarperCollins, 2001, 157
2. J.A.Houlding, *Fit for Service: The Training of the British Army 1715–95*, Oxford, Clarendon Press 1981, 6
3. ed: Peter Young, *History of the British Army*, London, Arthur Barker, 1970, 108; in 1801 the population of Great Britain was just under 11 millions.
4. D.S.Daniell, *Cap of Honour: The Story of the Gloucestershire Regiment*, London, Harrap, 1951, 77

Chapter 2
1. Piers Mackesy, *British Victory in Egypt 1801*, London, Routledge, 1995, 43,68; Carola Oman, *Sir John Moore*, London, Hodder and Stoughton, 1953, 258–60
2. Mackesy, 56, 62, 70–1
3. Daniell, 77

4 Moore's Journal quoted by Carola Oman, 260
5 Daniell, 78
6 Mackesy, 89
7 ibid, 88
8 ibid, 109, 112
9 Daniell, 81
10 Mackesy, 190,203
11 ibid, 159
12 T. Hay, *The Narrative of a Soldier* held at Soldiers of Gloucestershire Museum, Gloucester, 91–2
13 Mackesy, 226

Chapter 3

1 Charles Cadell, *Narrative of the Campaigns of the Twenty-Eighth Regiment*, London, Whittaker 1835, 2
2 ibid
3 G.C. Moore Smith (ed), *The Autobiography of Sir Harry Smith*, London, John Murray, 1910, 44
4 Bevan Papers (BP) Charles (C) – Mary (M) 27 May 1804
5 ibid
6 ibid, C-M 2 Sept 1804
7 ibid, C-M, 17 June 1804
8 ibid, C-M, 2 Sept 1804
9 ibid
10 Houlding, 100–1; Holmes, 160
11 M. Urban, *The Man who broke Napoleon's Codes*, London, Faber and Faber , 2001, 26
12 BP, C-M, 11 Nov 1804

Chapter 4

1 ed. F. Brodigan, *Historical Records of the Twenty-Eighth North Gloucestershre Regiment*, London, Blackfriars Printing, 1884, 44
2 L.Cowper, *The King's Own: the Story of a Royal Regiment*, Oxford University Press, 330, states that the 23rd, 26th and 28th were brigaded together. But Fortescue's *History of the British Army* v. 5, p.294, gives the 28th as being brigaded with the 26th and 91st under Maj-Gen Fraser. The probable explanation is that the 25th

moved across from Fraser's to Paget's division at Paget's request, as he particularly wanted his old regiment in his brigade.

3 Brodigan, 44
4 ed. I. Fletcher *In the Service of the King, the letters of William Thornton Keep*, Spellmount, Staplehurst, 1997, 128. Hebe, in Greek mythology the personification of Youth, was the daughter of Zeus and Hera, who was worshipped as the goddess of women and marriage.
5 Bevan Papers (BP) Charles (C) – Mary (M) 21, 24, 26 June 1807
6 ibid, C-M 26 June 1807; by 'excursion' is meant 'training'
7 Cadell, 10–11
8 ibid
9 Cowper, 337; for an account of the military campaign see ed. C. M. Woolgar *Wellington Studies II*, T.Munch Peterson 'Lord Cathcart, Sir Arthur Wellesley and the British attack on Copenhagen in 1807', Hartley Institute, University of Southampton 1999, 104–22
10 Carola Oman, 460
11 ed J. Sturgis, *A Boy in the Peninsular War: the Autobiography of Robert Blakeney*, London, John Murray, 1899, 18–19
12 Cowper, 339
13 Moore Smith, 15
14 BP, C-M, 30 June 1808
15 ibid, C-M, 21 June 1808
16 Cadell, 26–7
17 Cowper, 340, quoting Cadell

Chapter 5

1 G. M. Trevelyan, *History of England*, London, Longmans, 1944 ed., 583
2 Arthur Bryant, *The Years of Victory*, London, Collins, 1944, 205
3 Cowper, 342–3
4 Carola Oman, 518
5 Bevan Papers (BP), Charles (C)-Mary (M), undated October, 1808
6 ibid
7 BP,C-M, 11 October, 1808
8 Daniell, 100
9 Carola Oman, 520

10 Sturgis, 77
11 Cowper, 344
12 Christopher Hibbert, *Corunna*, London, Pan ed, 1972, 39
13 ibid
14 BP, C-M, 13 November, 1808
15 ibid
16 Cowper, 345
17 BP, C-M, 24 November, 1808
18 ibid
19 ibid
20 Hibbert, 82
21 ibid, 89
22 W. Napier, *History of the War in the Peninsula*, London, Warne, 1890 ed, Vol 1, 304. This gives Napoleon's forces as 60,000. To these must be added the 18,000 odd under Soult. Hibbert (at p.90) suggests the total figure of 80,000 which I have therefore used.

Chapter 6

1. See Napier, 315, 317, 319, 324; Bryant, 247, 254, 256; Hibbert 154
2. Sturgis, 114
3. Cowper, 356; but Sturgis, 115, states that the task was given to the 95th Foot
4. Napier, 328–32; Bryant, 260–1; Hibbert, 170–88; Daniell, 99–100

Chapter 7

1 Bryant, 294
2 Cowper, 362
3 Bevan Papers (BP), Charles (C)-Mary(M), 27 July, 1809
4 ibid
5 ed. F. Harvey, *The Oxford Companion to English Literature*, Oxford University Press, 1953, 531
6 G. C. Bond, *The Grand Expedition: The British Expedition to Holland 1809*, University of Georgia Press, USA, 1979, 105–6
7 ibid, 52
8 ibid, 76

9 BP, C-M, 12 August 1809

10 Bryant, 296; Bond, 96–7, 121

11 Bryant, 296

12 Hugh Popham, *A Damned Cunning Fellow*, Old Ferry Press, Tywardreath, 1991, 187. This book has an informative account of the Scheldt expedition.

13 Cowper, 363

14 BP, C-M, 12 August 1809

15 Bryant, 297

16 ed. Christopher Hibbert, *The Recollections of Rifleman Harris*, London, Leo Cooper, 1970, 115

17 Daniell, 101

18 Cowper, 361,365

19 Elizabeth Longford, *Wellington: The Years of the Sword*, London, Panther, 1976, 258

Chapter 8

1 John W. Fortescue, *A History of the British Army*, London, Macmillan, 1906–20 v. IV, 840

2 Cowper, 7–8

3 Bevan Papers (BP), Charles (C) – Mary (M), 12 February, 1810

4 Cowper, 368

5 Piers Mackesy, *The War in the Mediterranean 1803–10*, London, Longmans, Green, 1957, 268; according to Cowper (368–9) Wellington concluded a treaty with Spain whereby he undertook to garrison Ceuta and defend Portugal if the Spaniards would harass the French during the winter.

6 BP, C-M 26 March 1810

7 ibid, 15 April, 1810

8 ibid, 6 June, 1810

9 ibid, 8 April, 1810

10 ibid

11 ibid, 4 April, 1810

12 ibid, 21 July, 1810

13 John Grehan, *The Lines of Torres Vedras*, Spellmount, 2000, 94–7

14 Charles Oman, *A History of the Peninsular War*, Oxford, Clarendon Press, 1911, v. IV, 272

15 BP, C-M, 19 October, 1810
16 ibid, 3 Sept, 1810
17 ibid; see also letters written on 4 April, 24 August, 26 September and 18 November
18 ibid, 21 July, 1810
19 ibid, 8 August, 1810
20 ibid, 28 February, 1811
21 In Georgina Bevan's novel she has the 'very young' Julia carrying on in 1808 with her 'singing master', and consequently being sent, presumably to cool her heels, to her grandmother at Rottingdean. Charles goes and sees Nevitt to remonstrate with him about his behaviour. A year or so later in March 1809 comes the news of Julia's elopement. In the novel she now entirely disappears from the scene for a year and more, re-emerging in the summer of the following year, when Charles is at Ceuta; he hears about her from Caroline. In a short while there is news that Nevitt has deserted Julia, who is now pregnant. The next thing is that Charles, still at Ceuta, hears again that Julia has died in childbirth (in 1810 that is) and that she, Caroline, is adopting the baby. We cannot say just how accurate all this is, but we do know that Julia was still alive in 1811, so there may be other inaccuracies. Nevertheless this account is of considerable interest, fiction though it may be, because Georgina will have had family information not available to this author.

Chapter 9
1 Bevan Papers (BP), Charles (C)-Mary (M), 9 January,1811
2 ibid, C-M, 13 January, 1811
3 ibid, C-M, 9 July 1810, see also C-M 1 February 1810, 4 April 1810 and 3 September 1810
4 ibid, C-M, 13 January, 1811
5 Christopher Hibbert, *George IV*, London, Penguin ed, 1976, 359–62
6 Longford, 300
7 BP, C-M, 25 January 1811 and 8 February, 1811
8 J.Grehan, *The Lines of Torres Vedras*, Spellmount, 2000, 46, 49–66
9 ibid, 70

10 BP, C-M, 16 February, 1811
11 ibid, C-M, 1 February, 1811
12 ibid
13 ibid, C-M, 23 February, 1811
14 ibid, C-M, 8 February, 1811
15 M. Glover, *The Peninsular War 1807–14*, Penguin Books, ed. 2001, 143

Chapter 10

1. Bryant, 361; Glover, 143
2. Napier, v. III, 111–12
3. Charles Oman, v. IV, 139
4. ibid, 135
5. John Kincaid, *Adventures in the Rifle Brigade and Random Shots from a Rifleman*, Glasgow, Drew, 1909, 20
6. Grehan, 164
7. Napier, v.III, 119–21
8. Oman, v. IV, 152
9. Cowper, 376
10. Bevan Papers (BP), Charles (C) – Mary (M), 16 March, 1811
11. ibid, 27 March, 1811
12. Kincaid, 32
13. BP, C-M, 30 March, 1811
14. Napier, v.III, 131–3; Oman, v.IV, 191,195; Bryant, 368–9 Glover, 146–7
15. Oman, v.IV, 200
16. Horse Guards in Whitehall became the expression used to denote the army's high command. The Commander-in-Chief occupied an office overlooking Horse Guards Parade and St. James's Park
17. Information supplied by the Museum of the 15th/19th The King's Royal Hussars and Northumberland Hussars, Newcastle upon Tyne; F. J. Huddlestone *Warriors in Undress*, London, J. Castle, 1925, 18; Bryant, 365. 368–9, 382; Longford, 272, 323; Glover, 146, ,
18. S.G.P. Ward 'Brenier's Escape from Almedia, 1811', *Journal of the Society for Army Historical Research*, v.35, 1957, 23–35

Chapter 11

1. Glover, 148; the much earlier historian Napier, though, estimates Masséna's losses as 30,000 men.
2. Bevan Papers (BP), Charles (C) – Mary (M), probably 5 April, 1811
3. ibid, 15 April, 1811
4. W. O'Byrne, *A Naval Biographical Dictionary*, London, J. Murray, 1849, 256.
5. BP, C-M, 22 April, 1811. The reference to 'high treason' is obviously meant as a joke.
6. Charles Oman, v. IV, 301–6; these figures cited by Oman are also used by Longford, Glover and Grehan; *per contra* Napier puts Wellington's numbers at just over 33,000
7. ed. 2nd Duke of Wellington, *Supplementary Despatches, Correspondence, and Memorandum of Field Marshal the Duke of Wellington*, London, J Murray, 1858–64, v.VII, Wellington to Wellesley Pole, 15 May, 1811, 176
8. Oman, v.IV, 624, 630
9. BP, C-M, 9 May, 1811

Chapter 12

1. Napier, v. III, 154; Charles Oman, v. IV, 349
2. Oman, v. IV, 350; Marcellin Marbot *Memoires du General Marbot*, Paris, v. 2, 469–72, 474; Baron Fririon *Journal Historique de la Campagne de Portugal*, 214
3. Oman, v.IV, 351; Fortescue, v. XIV, 176
4. Murray Papers National Library of Scotland, Adv 46-4-16-126 and 127
5. ed.Lt-Col J Gurwood, *The Dispatches of Field-Marshal The Duke of Wellington*, London 1834–8, v.VII, Wellington to Liverpool, 15 May 1811, 562. Note Wellington sent both an official despatch and an unofficial letter to Liverpool on this date.
6. W. Verner, *History and Campaigns of the Rifle Brigade, 1809–1813*, London, Bale and Danielson, 1912–19, 91–3
7. Earl Stanhope, *Conversations with the Duke of Wellington* 1831–51, published privately 1888, 67; see also H. Maxwell *The Life of Wellington*, London, Sampson, Low and Marston, 1900, v. I, 232–3 quoting Tomkinson

8. Napier, v. III, 156; Fortescue, v. XIV, 178
9. ed Lt-Col J Gurwood, *The Dispatches of Field Marshal The Duke of Wellington*, London, J Murray, 1852 v.V, Appendix, Brenier to Marmont, 17 May 1811, 767–70 (note: this material does not appear in the 1834–38 ed)
10. ibid
11. ibid
12. ibid; we calculate that, given Brenier's march from Almeida to the bridge at Barba del Puerco was some 13 miles in length, then in order to reach the area of the bridge just before 6 am (his approximate time of arrival) he would have needed to travel at between 2 and 2½ miles per hour. Even if there was a moon, with a number of rivers to cross and unknown route to follow, this was a fair speed at which to march at night.
13. ibid, v. V. Campbell-Wellington, 12 May 1811, 14–15; Pack-Campbell, 12 May 1811 15–16
14. ibid, v.V, Pack – Campbell, 12 May, 1811, 15–16
15. Oman v. IV, 355; Fortescue, v. XIV, 177
16. ed Lt-Col J. Gurwood, *The Dispatches of Field-Marshal the Duke of Wellington*, London, 1852, v. V, Campbell – Wellington, 12 May 1811, 14–15
17. ibid; Oman, v. IV, 354; Marbot, op cit
18. Cowper, 380
19. Oman, v. IV, 355

Chapter 13

1. Bevan Papers, (BP) Charles-Mary, 15 May, 1811
2. Murray Papers, National Library of Scotland, ADV 46-2-12-220, letter from Bevan for transmission to Major-General Sir W. Erskine, 11 May, 1811
3. Ed. Lt-Col J. Gurwood, *The Dispatches of Field-Marshal The Duke of Wellington* (DW), 12 vols, London, J. Murray, 1834–8, v. VII, Wellington-Liverpool, 15 May, 1811, 562
4. Stanhope, 66
5. DW, v.VII, 565
6. Ed. J. Tomkinson, *Diary of a Cavalry Officer in the Peninsular and Waterloo Campaigns 1809–15*, London, 1894, 103

7. DW, v.VII, 565–6
8. Oman, v.IV, 353–356; Fortescue, v XIV, 178; Maxwell, 232; Cowper, 382
9. Napier, v.III, 156; Tomkinson, 102–3; G. Simmons *A British Rifleman: Journals and Correspondence during the Peninsular War*, London, Greenhill Books, 1986, 173–4; *Leaves from the Diary of an Officer of the Guards* (Anon), London, Trotman, 1994, 104–5
10. Ed. 5th Earl of Longford, *Pakenham Letters 1800–1815*, London, privately published 1914, (Hercules) Pakenham-Longford, 20 June 1811, 104
11. Longford, 316
12. BP, James Dacres-Charles Bevan (jnr), 13 July, 1843
13. Ward, 23–35
14. *The Army and Navy Gazette*, v. 29, 15 December 1888, 996
15. Stanhope, 66
16. Oman, v.IV, 353
17. Cowper, 379. In Richard Cannon's *Historical Record of the Fourth Regiment of Foot*, quoted by Cowper as a source, the author states that 'as the King's Own [the 4th Foot] were on the march to Barba del Puerco they heard the firing of musketry at a distance and hastened towards the scene of the conflict'.
18. Today it gets light in central Portugal in May at about 5.15 am depending on cloud. This is Greenwich Mean Time plus one hour. Therefore in 1811 it was beginning to get light an hour or so earlier.
19. Murray Papers, ADV 46-2-12-219, Erskine-Murray, 12 May, 1811
20. Tomkinson, 103
21. DW. v VII, 566
22. ibid, 563
23. ibid, 567
24. Tomkinson, 103
25. Pakenham Letters, (Hercules) Pakenham-Longford, 11 July 1811, 110
26. DW, v.VII, 566–7
27. Stanhope, 66
28. ed. 2nd Duke of Wellington, *Supplementary Despatches, Correspondence and Memoranda of Field-Marshal The Duke of Wellington*, London, 1858–64, v.VII, 123

29. Napier, v.III, 156; Oman, v.IV, 356; Fortescue, v.XIV, 178–9
30. Ward, op.cit
31. ibid, 33

Chapter 14
1. Bevan Papers (BP), Charles (C) – Mary (M) 28 May, 1811
2. BP, C-M, 19 June, 1811
3. Cowper, 381
4. Napier, v III, 315
5. *The London Gazette*, 28 May, 1811
6. ed, Eileen Hathaway, Costello: *The True Story of a Peninsular War Rifleman*, Shinglepicker Publications, Swanage, 1997, 125. A slightly different version of the jingle appears in Cowper at 382
7. *Pakenham Letters*, Pakenham-Longford, 11 July, 1811
8. Longford, 317
9. BP, J Dacres-Charles Bevan Jnr, 13 July, 1843
10. ibid
11. BP, C-M, 4 July, 1811. Colonel Williams was presumably also known to Mary. Charles' mother once had a house in Montague Square.
12. BP, J. Dacres-Charles Bevan Jnr, 13 July, 1843
13. ibid

Chapter 15
1. Bevan Papers (BP), – from notes made by Major Piper of 11 July, 1811
2. ibid
3. Oman, v. IV, 356; Cowper, 382. Not surprisingly the enemy heard that an officer blamed by Wellington for letting Brenier escape from Almeida, had committed suicide. Curiously there was confusion over his identity, and Marbot (at p. 478 of op.cit.) reported it was General Campbell who, having been brought before a court-martial, blew his brains out.
4. BP, J. Dacres-Charles Bevan Jnr, 13 July, 1843
5. Longford, 317–18
6. Andrew Roberts, *Napoleon and Wellington*, London, Weidenfeld and Nicolson, 2001, 38. Also see G. R. Gleig *The Life of Arthur Duke of*

Wellington, London, Longmans, Green, 1890, 1913; Huddleston, 18–20; Longford, 393; also see John Hussey in the *Journal of the Society for Army Historical Research* v.80 no.322, summer 2002, at 98–109. Hussey, in questioning Gleig's reliability, points out that the Army Lists continued to show Todd alive and well though on half pay after Waterloo.

7. Public Record Office, Kew, W.O.3/600, Torrens-Paterson 29 July, 1811
8. BP, Charles-Mary, 8 Feb, 1810
9. BP, J Dacres-Mary, 15 October,1811
10. BP, Mrs Dacres Snr-J. Dacres, undated, ca. 1823
11. BP, Charles Bevan Jr-J. Dacres, 11 July, 1843
12. BP, J. Dacres-Charles Bevan Jr, 13 July 1843
13. Newspaper cutting from a Cornish newspaper published at some time in 1872

Bibliography

Books are published in London unless stated otherwise.

Bond, G.C., *The Grand Expedition: The British Expedition to Holland, 1809*, University of Georgia Press, U.S.A., 1979

Brodigan, F. (ed.), *Historical Records of the Twenty-Eighth North Gloucestershire Regiment*, Blackfriars Printing, 1884

Bryant, Arthur, *The Years of Victory*, Collins, 1944

Cadell, Charles, *Narrative of the Campaigns of the Twenty-Eighth Regiment*, Whittaker, 1835

Cowper, L.I., *The King's Own: The Story of a Royal Regiment*, Oxford University Press, Oxford, 1939

Daniell, D.S., *Cap of Honour: The Story of the Gloucestershire Regiment, 1694–1950*, Harrap, 1951

Feiling, K., *A History of England*, Book Club Associates, 1972

Fisher, H.A.L., *A History of Europe*, Arnold, 1936

Fletcher, I. (ed.), *In the Service of the King, the Letters of William Thornton Keep*, Spellmount, Staplehurst, Kent, 1997

Fortescue, John W., *History of the British Army*, Macmillan, 1906–20

Fririon, Baron, *Journal Historique de la Campagne de Portugal*, Paris, 1841

Gleig, G.R., *The Life of Arthur Duke of Wellington*, Longmans, 1890

Glover, M., *The Peninsular War 1807–14*, Penguin Books, 2001

Grehan, John, *The Lines of Torres Vedras*, Spellmount, Staplehurst, Kent, 2000

Guedella, Philip, *The Duke*, The Reprint Society, 1940

Harvey, P. (ed.), *The Oxford Companion to English Literature*, Oxford University Press, Oxford, 1953

Hathaway, E. (ed.), *Costello: The True Story of a Peninsula War Rifleman*, Shinglepicker, Swanage, 1997

Henderson, James, *The Frigates*, Leo Cooper, 1994

Hibbert, C. (ed.), *The Recollections of Rifleman Harris*, Leo Cooper, 1970

Hibbert, C., *Corunna*, Pan, 1972

Hibbert, C., *George IV*, Penguin, 1976

Holmes, Richard, *Redcoat*, Harper Collins, 2001

Houlding, J.A., *Fit for Service: The training of the British Army 1715–95*, Clarendon Press, Oxford, 1981

Huddlestone, F.J., *Warriors in Undress*, Castle, 1925

Kincaid, John, *Adventures in the Rifle Brigade and Random Shots from a Rifleman*, Drew, Glasgow, 1909

Longford, 5th Earl of, *Pakenham Letters 1800–15*, privately published, 1914

Longford, Elizabeth, *Wellington: The Years of the Sword*, Panther, 1976

McGuffie, T.H. (ed.), *A Peninsular Cavalry General 1811–13: The Correspondence of* Lt. Gen. R.B. Long, Harrap, 1951

Mackesy, Piers, *The War in the Mediterranean*, Longmans, 1957

Mackesy, Piers, *British Victory in Egypt, 1801*, Routledge, 1995

Maloney, Linda, *The Captain from Connecticut*, Northeastern University Press, Boston U.S.A., 1986

Marbot, Marcellin, *Mémoires du Général Baron de Marbot*, Paris, 1892

Maxwell, Herbert, *The Life of Wellington*, Sampson Low and Marston, 1900

Moore Smith, G.C. (ed.), *The Autobiography of Sir Harry Smith*, Murray, 1910

Napier, Priscilla, *The Sword Dance*, Michael Joseph, 1971

Napier, William, *History of the War in the Peninsula*, Warner, 1890

O'Byrne, W., *A Naval Biographical Dictionary*, Murray, 1849

Officer of the Guards (anon), *Leaves from the Diary of an Officer of the Guards*, Trotman, 1994

Oman, Carola, *Sir John Moore*, Hodder and Stoughton, 1953

Oman, Charles, *A History of the Peninsular War*, Clarendon Press, Oxford, 1902–30

Popham, Hugh, *A Damned Cunning Fellow: the Eventful Life of Rear-Admiral Sir Home Popham*, Old Ferry Press, Tywardreath, 1991

Roberts, Andrew, *Napoleon and Wellington*, Weidenfeld & Nicolson, 2001

Simmons, G., *A British Rifleman: Journals and Correspondence during the Peninsula War*, Greenhill, 1986

Stanhope, Earl, *Conversations with the Duke of Wellington*, privately published in 1888

Sturgis, J. (ed.), *A Boy in the Peninsula War: the Autobiography of Robert Blakeney*, Murray, 1899

Tomkinson, J. (ed.), *Diary of a Cavalry Officer in the Peninsular and Waterloo Campaigns*, Spellmount, Staplehurst, Kent, 1999

Trevelyan, G.M., *The History of England*, Longmans, 1944

Urban, M., *The Man who broke Napoleon's Codes*, Faber, 2001

Verner, W., *History and Campaigns of the Rifle Brigade 1809–13*, Bale and Danielsson, 1912–19

Wellington, Gurwood, J. (ed.), *The Dispatches of Field Marshal The Duke of Wellington*, Murray, 1834–8 and 1852 eds.

Wellington, 2nd Duke of Wellington (ed.), *Supplementary Despatches, Correspondence and Memoranda of Field Marshal The Duke of Wellington*, Murray, 1858–64

Woolgar, C.M., *Wellington Studies II*, Hartley Institute, University of Southampton, 1999

Young, Peter and Lawford, J.P. (eds.), *History of the British Army*, Arthur Barker, 1970

Unpublished

Bevan Papers: in private ownership. Copy in the National Army Museum

Bevan, Georgina: "It may have happened thus: a chronicle of the courtship and married life of Charles Bevan, late Lt-Col of the 4th Regiment of Foot, and of Mary his wife". This novel is in private ownership

Hay, T.: "The Narrative of a Soldier" in Soldiers of Gloucestershire Museum, Gloucester

Murray Papers: National Library of Scotland (Department of Special Collections)

Public Record Office, Kew: W.O. 3/600

Records of 15th/19th The King's Royal Hussars, Newcastle-upon-Tyne

Records of the King's Own Royal Regiment, Lancaster

Records of the Gloucestershire Regiment, Gloucester

Published

The Army and Navy Gazette
Journal of the Society for Army Historical Research
The London Gazette

Index

210

211

212